Mindsets

Mindsets

The Role of Culture and Perception in International Relations

GLEN FISHER

Intercultural Press, Inc
Yarmouth, ME

For information contact
Intercultural Press, Inc.
P.O. Box 700
Yarmouth, Maine 04096
USA

Library of Congress No. 87-045836

Library of Congress Cataloging-in-Publication Data
Fisher, Glen, 1922-
    Mindsets: the role of culture and perception in international relations.

Bibliography: p.
    Includes index
    1. International relations and culture.   I. Title.
JX1255.F57   1988   327'.01'9   87-45836
ISBN-0-933662-67-X

Printed in the United States of America.

Contents

Preface

This book about "mindsets" is focused on the special kind of experience shared by people from all over the world who carry out their professional responsibilities in or relating to a foreign national or cultural environment. Their actual tasks may vary enormously, from establishing a cooperative clinic in a remote village to making a deal on a United Nations Security Council vote, from supervising local employees in an overseas operation to calculating threats and deterrents in national security affairs. What they have in common is that in addition to meeting the ordinary technical and institutional demands made of them by their professional commitment, they must find a way to cut through an extra layer of attitudes and psychological predispositions that would not be encountered if they were functioning in their home environments. They have to succeed or fail in their assignments in the context of some other society's hierarchy of concerns, priorities, and conventional wisdom. They work across contrasting mindsets—to use the term chosen here to lead into the discussion—but mindsets that have the special quality of reflecting differences in national experience and culture.

All this is a rather obvious fact of life in international relations, yet formal inquiry into the nature and effect of conflicting mindsets is rarely penetrating, usually given only passing attention in the study and analysis of international relations. This is true even though it is generally recognized that there are striking contrasts in international behavior which reflect religious, ideological, value, and institutional differences between nations and cultures, and even though anthropologists long ago established the link between culture and the way people perceive and think about the world.

When one considers the path by which international professionals acquire whatever level of diagnostic competence they have in this regard, it seems clear that effectiveness does not necessarily just come naturally from cumulative exposure and experience. In government programs, management and business, non-profit organizations, journalism, etc., the demand increases for a more systematic intellectual orientation for sorting out and dealing with all the unfamiliar patterns of perceiving, thinking and reacting that will be encountered. People who find themselves so engaged may not necessarily have planned for that on starting their careers. They may find that they have little to draw upon from their previous studies of engineering, management, government and politics, military affairs, finance, or whatever.

Even what might have been studied in routine undergraduate social science courses will often fail to come into focus as a resource for coping with foreign institutions and foreign peoples. The chapters that follow are intended to suggest a practical conceptual orientation for those who have not had occasion to delve into those social science disciplines that speak to problems of mindsets mismatched because of cultural differences. At the least, the intent is to set an agenda for what must be pursued in the inquiry.

This book is the culmination of a continuing special interest that started some years ago when, as a somewhat rare sociologist/ anthropologist in the career Foreign Service, I attempted to adapt conceptual tools from the behavioral sciences to meet the field needs of officers assigned overseas. This effort began in area study seminars at the State Department's Foreign Service Institute and continued in orientation programs in embassies abroad and, less formally, in discussions with anyone foreign or native who recognized my peculiar interest in these matters. At one point my interests led to a research assignment at the Fletcher School of Law and Diplomacy to study the way public beliefs and attitudes affect the foreign affairs process. (The resulting book, *Public Diplomacy and the Behavioral Sciences*, Indiana University Press, 1972, is now out of print.) A State Department policy assignment in its former Bureau of Educational and Cultural Affairs offered further opportunity for pursuing the subject, as do my current seminars at the Monterey Institute of International Studies.

In going back and forth between being practitioner and professor, it has seemed to me that educational and training programs have been only partly effective when they have tried simply to supply the facts regarding foreign concerns and outlooks. This kind of "briefing" approach is too limited. In the first place, our research and knowledge base in psycho-cultural matters is often too inadequate to offer reliable formulas. Secondly, the behavior of citizens of a given country is always in some degree less than uniform and predictable, especially in a time when a growing homogenized international culture reigns over much international interaction—at least superficially. The result is confusion in application. People involved need to develop an increased ability to probe into *why* standoffs caused by mindset differences exist. They need, to some extent, to be their own applied practical psychologists and anthropologists, whatever their specific skill or function.

The discussion ahead is intended to contribute toward that objective. It is task-oriented to a large degree; it is an exercise in *applied* social science. It does not pursue new knowledge, but questions how to use what we have. While much background literature has been consulted during this project, footnote citations will be confined to recognizing direct sources and noting resources for further exploration of subjects too briefly covered. Many of the examples that are used to illustrate points will come from the geographical areas of my own more sustained foreign experience. This means that Latin America, the Philippines, and various parts of the Far East will be mentioned more often.

It is assumed that most readers will be concerned with the international relations process because they are part of it in some way—which in final analysis includes almost everyone to be sure—or are preparing for international careers. It is hoped that readers will not be passive but will react to what is presented; any cross-cultural experience already accumulated can be used as personal "case study" material for trying out and expanding on ideas presented here. For students, exploring the psycho-cultural dimension of international affairs should be a worthwhile supplement to other more standard coursework.

In any event, the goal is to promote the sense of objectivity in dealing with mismatched mindsets which is demanded in an applied science. If the discussion here helps one to order observations when in an international environment or to develop a broader framework for making judgments in international activities, the purpose will be accomplished.

I would like to express sincere thanks for assistance from many quarters. My Foreign Service colleagues have very genially put up with my somewhat unconventional inquiry while we engaged in our diplomatic affairs workloads; sometimes they even made use of what I propounded! Students at the Monterey Institute of International Studies have struggled through earlier versions of the manuscript and have given me much-needed feedback from their own frequently substantial international experience. Lorita Fisher shared the Foreign Service experience with me, and from the vantage point of a Foreign Service wife often involved professionally in institutional and educational endeavors while overseas, contributed heavily in the production of the manuscript. David Hoopes and Margaret Pusch of the *Intercultural Press*, themselves professionals in the diagnosis of intercultural issues, have been friendly and insightful consultants beyond the duty of editors, as has been George Renwick of *Renwick and Associates*.

Mindsets

Dealing with Mindsets in International Affairs

One can hardly overstate the degree to which psychological and cross-cultural factors affect the international relations process today or the need for increasingly skilled and knowledgeable people to cope with them. The current degree of global interdependence alone means that many issues which at one time would have been resolved at home are now multi-national in nature. Whether it be managing governmental affairs, manufacturing and selling products, attending universities abroad, attacking pollution or producing media materials, many more people now have to communicate ideas internationally, interpret international events, judge intentions, work around suspicions and resentments, or cut through misperceptions. This is a not-to-be-dismissed challenge when the problem is international or cross-cultural.

Those who work internationally commonly find that all people are not necessarily led by the same evidence to the same conclusions. The televised picture of an airline hijacking will almost certainly have a different meaning for the average American than it has for the average Palestinian. A factory foreman in a country with a fatalistic view of the world will not be as preoccupied with preventive maintenance as one in Western Europe or the United States. When calculations of international strategy at the highest levels are based on such matters as credibility, deterrence, "sending messages" to one's adversaries, the perception of threat, human rights, or appeals to world opinion, it frequently turns out that assumptions held in one country regarding these matters are not matched in another.

Although we know this in a general way, our recognition of its full significance tends to be less than forthright. We too comfortably find ourselves relying on our domestic experience and normal ethnocentric common sense rather than focusing directly on new dimensions of problem-solving that are demanded by international realities. As occasions increase for international elbow-bumping because of a more mobile world population, faster and more pervasive communications technology, and the sheer volume of international business, so does the need to make better use of what is known about differing patterns of perceiving and reasoning—what we call the "mindset factor."

Using a term like "mindset" to probe the significance of psychological and cultural factors has certain advantages, even though it might not be the word of choice in more precise social science treatises. For one thing, its popular meaning is appropriate. Webster defines mindset as a "fixed mental attitude formed by experience, education, prejudice, etc." And that is exactly the dimension of the international relations process that concerns us—the reasons why people are predisposed to perceive and respond as they do.

Secondly, "mindset" is a middle-range kind of word, somewhere between jargon that is too technical and ordinary usage that fails to stimulate fresh thinking. "Mindset" is thus a useful conceptual tool for examining how people look at the specific events and problems that concern us in practical affairs. By being middle range in application, it does not require us first to encompass all the cognitive complexities impinging on the people whose perceptions we would understand or to establish all the elusive relationships between culture and personality, valuable though that might be for other purposes. Diagnosing mindsets as they relate to immediate problems is a more manageable objective.

"Mindset" has the further advantage of blending together a range of psychological considerations that derive both from the culturally related conditioning that will be stressed here and from the many other sources of psychological programming that we would not ordinarily call cultural, such as the immediate conditions of national and local life, unique individual experiences, or the content of modern media.

The conceptual framework will be enlarged upon in the next two chapters. The point for the moment is that those who work in or who closely follow international affairs need to develop competence in anticipating the way that persistent structures of the mind—mindsets—affect their international interaction. As many internationalists will not have prepared for such involvement before starting their careers, they may find that they now have to add something new to their arsenal of intellectual skills if they are to pursue their specialties and interests effectively across international boundaries.

This development of competence in analyzing mindsets across nations and cultures requires something more than simply studying languages or taking standard international relations or area study courses. Other approaches and skills are needed for making the judgments that specifically take into account the differing mindsets that make solving *international* problems so different from solving problems at home, where underlying assumptions, notions of reality, and habits of perceiving and reasoning can more or less be taken for granted as the cultural norm.

The task is more pressing when one is directly involved in international activities, in contrast to scholars or experts who enjoy the luxury of making *ex post facto* judgments. For despite all the foreign affairs knowledge accumulated in the academic mainstream, we are armed with relatively few systematic conceptual tools for managing the daily work routine where "international relations" actually takes place. The need to diagnose meaning, motive and intention on the spot and as events unfold is particularly great for those engaged in Foreign Service analysis and reporting, in negotiation, in gathering international news, conducting public diplomacy, pursuing economic development, conducting transnational business, or unraveling bureaucratic tangles between institutions that span national boundaries.

Unfortunately, in actual practice the practitioner too easily and naively assumes that such foreign mindset factors as need to be taken into consideration will be understood on the basis of one's previous experience in "understanding people" or in managing public relations. Normal ethnocentrism itself tends to produce self-assurance in this regard for both amateurs and professionals. The result is that the psychological dimension gets scant study or analytical attention from either foreign affairs experts or international practitioners.

Consequently, corporate managers step onto the plane for Saudi Arabia, Spain or Japan, fully confident that they can engage their counterparts in effective negotiation without even minimal psycho-cultural briefings. Or a Congressional delegation goes on a two-day foreign fact-finding mission, assured that seeing for themselves will give them a grasp of the issues. Students enroll in foreign university programs with little concern for any contrasts in the academic cultures they are entering.

This book is intended to speak to the needs of not just Foreign Service Officers and others mentioned above involved in formal diplomatic relations, but journalists, business executives, technical assistance personnel, international governmental and non-governmental organization professionals, volunteers, educators, and scholars and students who think of themselves as part of the international relations process.

The thesis here is that in order to make sense out of the bits and pieces of interaction that make up routine international workloads, it is often as important to anticipate the way *those involved are programmed to perceive the issue at hand* as to understand the formal substance of the issue, important though that may be. Few principal actors on the foreign scene make decisions by cold logic or completely "rational" analysis, and certainly their publics and clients do not—in itself an increasingly important consideration in today's public and business affairs. For example, suppose that the historical background of a given issue or event was necessary to understand its significance. While it may be important to check the historical facts, *knowing how that history is remembered* may be more to the point in planning a negotiating position or choosing an effective policy than the actual events because that will be the *operative* history.

To be realistic, then, one must pursue "reality" in international activities very cautiously. It is fundamental that people, including those on one's own side of an issue, do not ordinarily react to an event or issue on the basis of the facts as might be empirically determined, but on the basis of their images of the facts, on what they think or believe to have happened or to have been at stake. Thus, international relations revolve around an interplay of images.[1]

Or perhaps better said, when reduced to routine conduct of business, international relations is basically a communication process and therefore a function of differing mindsets, i.e., the differing ways that the subject at hand is perceived, understood, or reasoned about. Notwithstanding, it is precisely this variable that is too often left out. Mindsets may be as relevant in a foreign affairs calculation as an inventory of development resources or a point of international law. In security affairs, unquantifiable emotions, embedded antagonism, or a particular sense of purpose might count for more than numbers of weapons or neatness in the chain of command.

Even in professional work at home, most people recognize a mindset dimension when they have to deal with differing points of view or sets of priorities. Managing these matters might simply be considered a question of expected competence. The trouble is that the informal understanding which one may have absorbed by experience in dealing with the human factor in one society can actually prove a liability in another unless that competence, often subconscious, can be adapted to a foreign perceptual and reasoning environment.

Mastering the gap between national mindsets will not necessarily bring peace and resolve all problems and issues. Indeed, a clear understanding of such contrasting outlooks as are involved might make basic conflicts all the more obvious. Paying more attention to the mindset factor should, however, at least help cut down the damage caused by *misperception*. The anxiety that is created by confronting the unknown and unpredictable can be reduced when "foreign" behavior is understood in terms of its particular logic and rationality. To the extent that the subject matter at hand is concrete—petroleum production or a manufacturing process, for example—the probability of misperception is reduced, of course. Correspondingly, the more abstract the issue, as in questions of political policy, law and morality, or projects and plans, the greater the potential mismatch in perception and reasoning, and therefore in communication. In any case, unrecognized and unresolved disjointed images quickly compound the difficulty in the interaction and communication process.

In the lore of those who have lived and worked abroad there are countless tales of cross-cultural snarls in communication in which misattributed motives or conflicts in perception have created havoc, even when the will to cooperate was present. I recall spending an entire day trying to ease a standoff resulting from out-of-phase mindsets between the Governor of a Bolivian province and the project manager of an American highway construction firm. The American, in hopes of improving strained public relations, had offered the use of a bulldozer to help construct a city park. The Governor was to supply the fuel, which was delayed. In the meantime, an unexpected need for the equipment for a short job developed elsewhere, and with only that as an explanation, the manager started to remove the bulldozer from the park project. The Governor jumped to his own conclusions; one misperception led to another. My task became one of trying first to convince the Governor that the American's intention was purely one of efficiency and not a slap at the Governor's inability to supply the fuel on schedule, and then to convince the American that the Governor would, in fact, send in an army group to prevent the bulldozer's transfer. The American had to be persuaded that such action would not be seen locally as extreme, but reasonable, given the insult to a Bolivian ego and the degree to which the Governor's prestige was on the line after having announced that the park project was a sure thing. (Such functions of Foreign Service Officers are not ordinarily well covered in textbook descriptions of diplomacy!)

Another example comes from the world of international personnel management. In this case a U.S. Information Agency Officer found himself dependent on diplomatic immunity to exit the Philippines for home leave in the face of a law suit brought against him by one of his former local employees. The problem stemmed from a breach of expected role behavior—a key element in supervisor-employee relations—and from subsequent incorrect projections of motives onto each other.

When the American first arrived, he understood from his predecessor that their senior local employee, a former journalist, was exceptionally competent, which he translated into an image of a person who could take initiative and handle innovative projects. But that image did not take into account the expected deference to specific instructions which, as seen from the employee's side, was considered proper in American superior and Filipino subordinate working relationships. Slow response by the Filipino to repeated general suggestions that new initiatives be drafted was interpreted as laziness, stubbornness, even resentment toward his new supervisor. Subsequent accusations to this effect violated the Filipino's sense of personal dignity even more than might be expected in a similar situation in the United States. In the end, it all led to the discharge of an employee who, by Philippine practice, had been exceptionally loyal and productive. The public, of course, sided with the discharged employee after the issue had been aired in the local press. There was a call for legal action. The result was unnecessary damage to public relations, a loss of useful talent, lingering confusion on the part of the rest of the local staff, and many months later, a personally embarrassing delay in the officer's departure for home.

An example of the mindset factor at work at the highest level of international affairs is the sequence of events in 1979 in which the American Embassy in Teheran was attacked and its diplomatic personnel held hostage after the deposed Shah of Iran was admitted to the U.S. from Mexico for medical treatment. That Iranians could defy all existing international precedent for respecting a foreign embassy was seen as highly irrational action. To Americans, both the Iranian government (to the extent that it was in control) and the militants who prolonged the situation month after month, were viewed as primitives in a modern world. Just defining the action as an "embassy takeover" placed the perpetrators outside the limits of civilized behavior.

The contrast in mindsets between Americans and Iranians was so great that bridging them was almost impossible, as was implied in a tongue-in-cheek remark made in the State Department: "You see, Jack, it is all a matter of the Gods. Now ours is a nice, reasonable, rational kind of a God. But the Ayotollah Khomeini's God—he's crazy!" However that might be, this was a case in which contrasts in perceptions regarding the nature of a diplomatic mission, the reasons for admitting the Shah, the causes of Iranian troubles, spying and espionage, and the U.S. role in the world, were as deep and unreconcilable as are likely to be found in international relations. The chain of events was exceptionally dramatic.

The question that was much debated after the hostages were finally released was whether this severe jolt to the course of American foreign relations could have been avoided by more accurately diagnosing the psychological forces at work in Iran and thus anticipating the nature and strength of Iranian reaction to the Shah's presence on American soil. Those on the scene in Iran and reporting to Washington certainly were able to foresee the direction and to some extent the intensity of the reaction. But those who made the decisions in Washington clearly were not. This case is all the more poignant because among those who urged the Shah's admission were the "best and brightest" of 1979, the acclaimed "experts" in the conduct of foreign affairs, including former Secretary of State Henry Kissinger. An ethnocentric President Carter was unable to evaluate conflicting advice; his problems were compounded by misinformation which made it appear that the medical necessity for treatment in the United States was greater than it turned out to be. The point to ponder is this: the decision-making apparatus of a country that provides leadership for the international community was unable to break out of its conventional mold of thinking to take into account the basic, if very foreign, psychological reality on which all else depended, and therefore was unable to anticipate consequences that it almost certainly would have avoided if possible.[2]

In retrospect, one can see at least some basis for contrasting perceptions of the Shah's admission "for medical treatment." On the U.S. side was the sovereign assumption that the U.S. could admit whomever it chose, and, in fact, one would have had to present a strong case to deny such a request. Further, whatever the Shah's faults, he had been friend and ally, and the U.S. did not want to risk credibility (that psychologically loaded word) by turning its back on that relationship. There was a felt obligation. With a life at stake, medical treatment was assumed to be better in the U.S. than in Mexico—a provincial and ethnocentric outlook to be sure, but given the history of medical advance, an understandable mindset. Perhaps most important, the action was defined in U.S. thinking in *humanitarian*, and, therefore, in politically neutral terms; this, it was calculated, would *naturally* be understood in Iran.

Iranian mindsets differed profoundly. To start with, there was a hyperanxiety that the U.S. would engage in some kind of action to return the Shah to power. This seemed to be the logical ulterior purpose of the Shah's presence in New York. To the Iranian public the memory of the Shah's initial assumption of power included an element of American connivance; hence, the Iranian outlook could logically assume that U.S. intentions were hostile enough to the success of the Iranian revolution that an attempt would be made to reverse it. Added to that was the desire to take retribution against the Shah for the repression experienced under his regime—and an antipathy toward anyone who was seen to have contributed to it. Thus, the U.S. was identified with the Shah's regime, the destruction of which was what the revolution was all about. The situation invited a preoccupation with plotting and spying. It had not escaped notice that the American Embassy, that "den of spies," had in fact been headed not long before by a former director of the Central Intelligence Agency (Richard Helms). Further, the revolutionary world view in Iran was based on a particular set of Islamic religious assumptions that made little provision for respecting modern international diplomatic traditions. Hence, despite the Islamic cultural tradition of hospitality toward guests, the Iranian mindset at that time left the American establishment very vulnerable.

All this is not to judge behavior on either side, but to note its basis and suggest that in cold calculation of one's own national interest, the reaction to the Shah's admission to the U.S. could have been more competently estimated. In a day and age when analytical skills are so highly developed in other managerial and technical fields, a higher level of sophistication surely must be attainable in dealing with the psychological realities that underlie the behavior of governments and their publics in relation to issues. There was really little "irrational" action on either side in this case; action and reaction did fit into a design of implicit assumptions, salient concerns, and a context of other events and problems. But the reciprocal "rationality" of action would not be appreciated without a studied review of the contrasting bases from which perceptions and reasoning derived.

The irony is that in 1986, with six years to digest the lessons of this case, the Reagan administration displayed even less sophistication in dealing with Iran in trying to exchange arms for hostages, producing a crisis at home and undercutting confidence in U.S. foreign policy leadership abroad.

EXPLORING MINDSETS IS A TWO-WAY STREET

The Iran hostage case is especially important in that by dominating a full year of U.S. international relations and by presenting so dramatic a contrast in psycho-cultural factors, it stimulated a new wave of concern for competence in this aspect of international relations analysis and policy formulation. For instance, the State Department's Foreign Service Institute was promptly directed to augment the social and cultural analytical content of their training courses for political reporting officers, the resources for which were not as readily available as one might imagine.

It also demonstrated the need to take a *comparative* approach in trying to understand what was going on. The problem, in attempting to explain the disastrous standoff, was not simply one of comprehending the alien outlooks of the Iranian revolutionaries but of understanding the American mindset as well. This kind of detached objectivity is extraordinarily hard to achieve. As will be explained further in Chapter III, normal socialization into one's own culture leads one to adopt, *out of awareness*, many of the fundamental elements of one's own mindset and to accept these as "common sense," even as human nature. As the officer said, our God is reasonable, Khomeini's is crazy! Our perception of our Embassy's practice is the human and universal one, theirs is bizarre. This naive approach feels good, of course, but it does not go very far in helping people make accurate diagnoses of what is going on in an international communication event.

It should be noted, therefore, that throughout our discussion of mindsets, the two-way nature of the inquiry will be fundamental. Indeed, most international problems involve perceptions and reactions from more than two parties to an action, from more than a simple dyad of cultural or sub-cultural identities. This is an added complication even before considering the variation among individuals. This comparative approach is common in analytical social science disciplines. One probes by establishing the mindsets on both sides.

THE IMPORTANCE OF PUBLIC PERCEPTIONS

The Iran case also forces one to examine the role that the public's understanding of international events and problems plays in determining the way issues are joined and resolved. Clearly, we have ever increasing reason to consider public mindsets. Even in diplomacy, today's reality in foreign affairs is found less in the formal dimension of diplomatic practice and more in the informal and even "irrational" dimension which involves selective knowledge, prejudices, attitudes, and opinions of participating masses of people. The all-encompassing reach of today's communication media is an obvious and essential contributor and is itself a subject of increasing attention in world affairs. There is now a much more pervasive public awareness and knowledge of world events and a much more insistent identification with them even in remote areas.

And the media, rather than being simply the conveyor of information about international events, has with increasing frequency become part of them. The Iran case was a media and public event from beginning to end. The militants holding the American hostages tried, with considerable success, to bypass the U.S. Government, using television as a bridge to reach the American public directly and gain its sympathy. As it turned out, they miscalculated the effect of their message and, rather than gaining leverage, they increased the sense of outrage in the U.S. In turn, the feeling among Americans of having participated in the trauma along with the hostages led to intensified public reaction and a media extravaganza when the hostages were finally released. Incredibly, an American fiasco in international affairs turned into a hero's welcome for the victims and an occasion for renewed patriotism.

The perceptions of the American public were also a precipitating factor in the course of events that removed President Ferdinand Marcos from the Philippine political scene in 1986 after the fraudulent nature of his re-election was broadcast around the world. With very heavy media coverage and a story that had extraordinary appeal to the American sense of how elections ought to be conducted, the U.S. Congress and finally the Reagan administration, pushed at least in part by American public reaction, signaled support for the legitimacy of rival Corazon Aquino's cause. This, via media feedback, encouraged the Philippine public to confront the Marcos forces and gave heart to dissident military officers who were crossing over to the Aquino side.

Vietnam, an earlier case, was something of a turning point in the history of how public perceptions have become, in modern times, an increasingly integral element in the working out of international events. Public support for U.S. involvement in Vietnam was turned around by the war being brought into the living rooms of the American public via television. The impact was so powerful that it not only constituted a major contribution to the U.S. withdrawal from Vietnam but negatively affected public attitudes toward the soldiers who had fought there.

The point is that the importance of public mindsets in international relations has increased much faster than our analytical attention to them. Greater public involvement changes the way the international process works. In business and diplomacy, for example, decision makers and negotiators find that their range of alternatives is constrained by the moods and viewpoints of their interested publics. They must work as hard to find the points of agreement that will sell at home as to find those that will convince their counterparts abroad—and the publics to which their counterparts must appeal. The negotiation of the Panama Canal treaty in 1978 was a notable instance. The Carter Administration made a strong and concerted effort to explain to the public why the traditional American outlook on the canal had to give way to new circumstances.

Diplomatic attention today centers somewhat less on foreign offices, negotiating tables and conference rooms, and more on the streets and television screens where the outlooks of masses of people are formed. Diplomats depend less on traditional practices in which emotion is set aside, where parties to negotiation refer to their position papers and deal with counterparts who share an established logic regarding international issues and the way to negotiate them. The precisely written message, the appeal to precedence and international law used to count for more. Those involved had a greater ability to agree on the facts and come to common definitions of obtainable objectives.[3]

There has been a growing attempt to take public opinion into international relations calculations, to be sure. There has long been propaganda in wartime. In the post-World War II years, the United States Information Agency has become well established along with similar government operations in other countries. But however effective these activities might be in persuading foreign audiences, the growing importance of public outlooks for the international relations processes poses a new kind of challenge for foreign affairs managers: choosing policies and programs in the first place which can be expected to gain their objectives because consideration was given *in advance* to public perception and reaction factors. Trying to manipulate public opinion afterwards is too little and too late. Probable public perceptions of policies and actions have to be accurately assessed at the policy deliberation stage, not merely at the public relations stage after the fact.

GOING BEYOND USUAL ACADEMIC APPROACHES

Certainly there is no shortage of foreign affairs analysts, whatever their qualifications, nor of textbooks to prepare the novice.

International relations is a standard discipline in colleges and universities. Scholarly attention is given to it in graduate schools. There are associations and journals. Indeed, few subjects command so extensive a literature, ranging from daily editorials to carefully researched history to abstruse contemporary theory. Yet, at least where academic and scholarly production is concerned, there is a substantial gap between what the specialists write about and the problems faced by practitioners on the ground.

The analytical environments in which practitioners and scholarly specialists work are very different, especially in time frames imposed upon each for the collection and processing of information, and in the audience each is expected to address. It is one thing to write for other scholars, or even for the public, from a long-range perspective and with ample time to fine-tune one's analyses. It is another to report to decision makers who have to manage an interplay of extraordinarily diverse considerations in deciding what to do about a particular problem, and then to orchestrate that decision with other policies and actions that are related in one way or another, all within a matter of hours or days—or, at best, weeks.

Academic resources sometimes seem irrelevant because the academic specialist has the luxury of examining foreign affairs decisions from the outside looking in, while the practitioner sees international affairs from the inside looking out. One consequence is that the big decisions scholars write about are usually not seen from the inside as single decisions at all, but as a series of smaller ones which, added together, become the historical events that are the grist for the international studies mill.[4]

The intervention in Vietnam is a case in point. Of the long series of decisions made by separate parts of the government, most appeared (to those who made them) to be sensible at the time and in the context of their immediate concerns. Added together, however, the cumulative effect was a much less sensible decision—increasing involvement in the conflict.

Paul Kattenberg's *The Vietnam Trauma in American Foreign Policy, 1945-75*[5] is a penetrating study of this phenomenon; all along the way, decisions were understandable given the circumstances, perceptions and personalities. The end result, however, was the national "trauma" that Vietnam became. As both a participant in the events as a Foreign Service Officer and a political scientist specializing in Southeast Asia, Kattenberg has been able to analyze Vietnam from a combined perspective: outside looking in and inside looking out.

It is our contention that for all the accomplishments in foreign affairs analysis, neither the international relations discipline nor the other social sciences has been able to pragmatically present a coherent set of conceptual tools to help the practitioner be his or her own political scientist, communications specialist, social psychologist or anthropologist. This failure results in part, no doubt, from the fact that the problems practitioners face cannot be packaged to fit neatly into any one of the disciplines as institutionalized in academia. Whatever the cause, they have been given little to help them in defining what they need to know in situations to which, formally or informally, they must apply their own powers of observation as actual participants in order to analyze psychocultural considerations—and take responsibility for their decisions. In any case, practitioners cannot wait to act until a scholarly research project has been carried out to support their diagnosis of a situation.

A half-dozen generalizations will be offered here to sum up this scholar-practitioner gap:

1. Much of the analysis produced in international relations circles focuses on the tips of the international relations icebergs. That is, observers and analysts not directly involved in the practice of international affairs tend to be most attracted to the highly visible issues: newsmaking events, strategic policies, causes of war, or the performance of high-level decision makers. But this distorts the reality of international relations. Most of the activity and most of the work on international tasks takes place below the waterline, where most of the iceberg lies hidden from view. Also, the real international relations process is far more encompassing than simple political relations among governments. A large number of nongovernmental institutions also play an increasingly important part: business, professional associations, nonprofit organizations, religious institutions, even athletic teams. Thus, those who read *Foreign Affairs* or who have gone through a traditional academic international relations program, may have a strong and accurate sense of context and background but may, at the same time, be ill-prepared to make judgments in specific or routine problem situations.

2. Even the most thoroughly researched analyses made by *single-discipline* specialists, such as political scientists or economists, also seem to distort reality, for a practitioners concerns are intrinsically multidisciplinary. That is, they are political, economic, social, psychological, technical and usually cross-cultural all at the same time. The well-prepared candidates for working in this kind of arena would be people carrying a methodology in their heads that is interdisciplinary and an intellectual capacity for integrating all the diverse incoming information and interplay of pressures that bear on the problem at hand. The degree to which academics resist engaging in interdisciplinary inquiry, or even crossing disciplinary lines in their personal intellectual development, tends to reduce their potential contribution to understanding specific issues set in specific times and places.

3. There is, in fact, a contrast in ultimate purpose between the scholar and the practitioner. The former is engaged in *explaining,* usually after the fact, while the latter, in the midst of a dynamic situation, is engaged in *estimating consequences* of alternative actions. While related, these are essentially different skills. Further, while the scholar's audience ranges from other scholars and the interested public to—in a rather disembodied way—the policy makers, the practitioner's audience includes both colleagues and antagonists directly engaged in actions that, taken together, become the event that scholars and pundits study.

4. There is a question to be raised regarding academic "ivory towers" and the *level of abstraction* at which academic international relations specialists have pursued their analytical efforts. During the decade of the 1970s the level of abstraction was often very high, dealing with the international system itself and the interaction of forces and factors within it. Models, paradigms and simulations were essential to analysis, especially as quantifiable relationships were sought. (An example of an inquiry that never went very far: Does the level of U.S. foreign aid correlate with revolutions in Latin America?) At the same time, research subjects were often chosen at the lowest level of abstraction, not because they were important, but because they were useful for testing methodology. I recall the scholar who, to the delight of Foreign Service Officers, established after meticulous research that members of the press were more in favor of having the State Department release information to the

press than were State Department officers! While all this scholarly effort has an understandable rationale in terms of developing international relations as a social science discipline, it has left those working at the middle range of abstraction—that is, those working at the process level rather than at either the structure-and-system end or the isolated event level—profoundly unimpressed. It has been of little utility, if the practitioner followed it at all.

5. On the other hand, while less preoccupied with methodology, much of the foreign affairs analysis produced by journalists and other less academic specialists in the foreign affairs community is often too specific-event oriented or specific-issue centered. What is learned in one case is not necessarily transferable to the next. The danger is that the conclusions reached in one case, however accurate, tend to be carried over by analogy into the next, so that we find ourselves refighting the old wars or projecting old assumptions onto new problems.

Using the experience and knowledge of these analysts and commentators is an enormous asset in building an informed public and in advancing the deliberation process in a democratic society, but this does not necessarily constitute a "disciplined" inquiry. It is necessary to distinguish competent and valid analysis from biased advocacy and politically-motivated exhortation which reflects ethnocentric assumptions about issues deriving from the national mindset of the moment. Some critics suggest, for example, that both the Soviet analysts who cover developments in the United States and American specialists who analyze Soviet affairs—and some social scientists too—tend to cruise along on the inertia of rather rigid assumptions arrived at years before, and in the process miss the meaning of contemporary events and changes in the two societies. Understanding Gorbachev's reforms in the USSR or the changing role of organized labor in the U.S. would pose this kind of reciprocal dilemma.[6]

THE PRACTICAL VARIABLE: THE WAY PEOPLE DEFINE AND UNDERSTAND ISSUES

Basically, the problem posed in working cross-nationally is to determine the way in which a task is unique precisely because it *is* international rather than domestic. Of all the factors which make international working situations unique, the differing ways that the parties involved perceive the problem at hand and reason about measures to be taken relative to it are the most troublesome. The common sense or obvious consideration domestically becomes not so common or obvious internationally. The ability to predict is greatly reduced. The convincing explanation falls flat. Politics, that "art of the possible," responds to a differing set of assumptions. What is right and wrong, reasonable and unreasonable, takes on differing coloration. Institutions operate on differing logic.

One obvious place to start looking for the solution to this problem is in the contrasts in mindsets that underlie the variations in behavior one encounters in an international environment. This is the loose cannon on the deck or, to be more erudite, the key but elusive variable, and demands that we look at ways that minds on both sides are programmed to process the subject matter at hand. The search, to be useful, is for probable differences in *patterns* within mindsets and the psychological realities that typically go with differences in culture and national experience.

In part, differing perspectives are to be anticipated simply by virtue of the uniqueness of a country's national experience, by its particular history (and, as noted, by the way it is remembered), economic concerns, political processes, etc. Even when these matters are given adequate consideration as explanation for mindsets, they are only partial explanations, for they tend to leave out cross-cultural analysis as we normally think of it. To arrive at a more complete understanding of the importance of differing perspectives, we have to take into account not only the kinds of "national" experience noted above, but also factors usually seen as falling within the province of cultural anthropologists or cross-cultural psychologists: traditional assumptions, religion, folk philosophy, values, perceptual systems, child-rearing practices, and so forth.

Psychological issues are being increasingly addressed in the international studies field, especially as related to decision makers and the decision-making process, and the study of conflict and conflict resolution (there is a publication entitled *Journal of Conflict Resolution*). Conflicts such as those in Cyprus and the Middle East have been explored in their psychological dimensions. Salient world personalities have invited psychological and even psychiatric analysis at a distance. Psycho-biographies have been written about Luther, Hitler, Gandhi, and Lawrence of Arabia, for instance. Cold

War propaganda and U.S.-Soviet ideological competition have spawned a number of psychological studies. Much of the early work in this area was summed up in 1965 in a well-known book edited by Herbert Kelman, *International Behavior: A Social Psychological Analysis.*[7]

More recently scholars have begun to examine the "operational codes" by which decision makers meet issues and problems, attempting, in effect, to chart the cognitive processes at work in their minds as they define and respond to issues.[8] Stanford University's Alexander George looks to the psychological processes which affect quality of reasoning in his *Presidential Decision-making in Foreign Policy: The Effective Use of Information and Advice.*[9] He sees the course of international relations often riding on how leaders use the information available to them in the light of (1) their existing beliefs and images and (2) their ability to objectively program their mental processes to define the context and meaning of new events and/or to try to understand an opponent's perspective.

In his *Nations in Darkness,* John Stoessinger offers a provocative study of how misperceptions—in the minds of the public as well as their leaders—have pervaded the major positions the U.S., Russia and China have taken vis-a-vis one another. The way that Americans have selectively perceived the virtues of Chiang Kai-shek is an example of a public fixation that has persisted to this day.[10]

Some attention has been given to the way that group processes reinforce collective unexamined assumptions in the course of reaching decisions, as is clearly signaled in the title of Irving Janis's book *Victims of Group-think.*[11] This subject will be discussed in more detail later on. Perhaps the most systematic inquiry into the psychological dimensions of international relations has been undertaken by Robert Jervis in his *Perception and Misperception in International Politics,*[12] a study that demonstrates the applicability of specific theories and propositions in psychology to decision making. (Again, it is not cross-cultural in approach, and is more of a scholarly tour de force than a guide for the practitioner.)

Where does all this leave the nonscholars who, whether by career design or not, find themselves international practitioners? They do have available a rich literature that covers the international system and the structure of international relations and that provides competent descriptions and analyses of particular events.

They also have the resources, just discussed, which examine international relations from a relatively abstract psychological perspective. What is less available is an applied science that pertains to the process by which individuals and institutions actually *conduct* their international business. The result is that for most practitioners, foreign affairs expertise becomes a matter of accumulated experience.

The challenge, then, is to make the cumulative experience applicable to new problem situations. Does the old hand have twenty years' experience or one year's experience twenty times? Is there some intellectual approach by which one becomes a keener and more organized observer, by which one is surer of what one is looking for in making sense out of cross-cultural situations, by which experience does in fact become cumulative?

In search for answers to these questions, our next step will be to review some of the basics in perception psychology as they apply to international matters. This will be undertaken in Chapter Two. Following that, in Chapter Three, the concept of culture will be explored for what it tells us about mindsets and how they work. In Chapter Four we will try to bring some of the main points together in a checklist that will be a helpful guide to diagnosing a standoff in mindsets in an actual situation.

We will draw heavily on precedent in the following pages. But there will be three main differences in the approach used here. First, there will be an insistence on seeking cross-societal and cross-cultural explanations for problems arising in international dialogue. Second, we will place more emphasis on the *patterns* of perceiving and reasoning that characterize cultural and national groups than on the unique qualities of individual leaders. And third, we will suggest approaches that can be used as conceptual tools by nonacademic professionals in day-to-day practice rather than as instruments of academic research.

The Psychological Process: Perception and Reasoning

"Mindsets," as we have noted, is more of a popular than a technical word for discussing how contrasts in habits of perception and patterns of reasoning affect give-and-take on the international scene. Yet we propose using it, for although it covers a rather diffuse range of psychological considerations, its popular meaning and usage give a good initial idea of the difficulties we wish to address and the international communication problem that needs to be understood better. Also, it is easy to apply the mindset idea to the everyday subject matter with which we deal. People do draw on differing mindsets when thinking about how an economy should work, how young people should be educated, the way that U.S. actions affect the rest of the world, or even what constitutes the good life.

But we need to flesh out just what we mean by mindsets and think through what they are and how they work. So this chapter invites readers to review the fundamentals of social psychology and consider how principles of perception and reasoning apply to international interaction problems.[1] The prospect of everyone playing amateur psychologist may be a little frightening, yet we all do make psychological judgments when engaged in international activities, whether naively or with some notion of what we are doing.

The psychological phenomenon we are trying to identify when we talk about mindsets will stand out more clearly if we note other terms which the reader may have encountered or used before to refer to some aspect of the process by which a person invokes a preset formula for thinking about a subject. A common thread runs through the following:

attitude

stereotype

idée fixe

prejudice

world view

definition of the situation

thought pattern

image

cognitive set

cognitive map

operational code

perception habit

mental construct

"Where a person is coming from"

If we put all these together and come back to mindsets, we see that we are concerned with predispositions to perceive and reason in certain ways. If one of the core difficulties in dealing with international issues derives from this kind of pre-programming, then some of the psychologist's basic ideas regarding perception and reasoning need to be applied.

Happily, this is a reasonably straightforward exercise. Whether one has gone over this ground in introductory psychology classes or not, these ideas are congenial to common vocabulary and usage. When we use expressions like, "the way the senator perceived the problem..." or "what a strange line of reasoning!" our psychological vocabulary is adequate, at least for a start.

So the question now is, what are the points that psychologists would make for our consideration?

1. *Some kind of design for perceiving and reasoning is indispensable.* In pursuing problems created by misperception in international affairs, it is easy to think of mindsets as barriers to appropriate reactions to reality and, therefore, as something to deplore and remedy. But the ability to develop an efficient and coherent mental cross-referencing system is not only constructive, it is phenomenally productive when viewed from the perspective of human evolution. It would be a limited psyche indeed that would have to

process each new stimulus as it came along without reference to past experience. The human mind simply cannot encompass the full complexity of all the events and stimuli which press upon it from even its own immediate, everyday environment, much less a radically expanded international environment. It must therefore have a means of efficiently screening, sorting, coding and storing sensory data. This need is met by structuring experience, for example, by establishing categories within which we can pigeon-hole given ranges of phenomena which concern us.[2] Thus, we have ways of interrelating experience and giving it meaning. At one level we adopt words and phrases to designate given slices of our experience or our physical surroundings—for growing plants: trees, grass, shrubs; for powered wheeled vehicles: automobiles, trucks, busses; for people engaged in government: politicians, senators, civil servants.

Mindsets, then, are to larger issues what words are to the specifics—a means of simplifying the environment and bringing to each new experience or event a pre-established frame of reference for understanding it.

Because this environment includes other people, and because any infant has to learn from other people how to survive, there is both a need and a basis for similarity in the cognitive structures adopted by members of a group, so that everyone who has to cooperate "simplifies" the environment in the same way. Consequently, we have culture.

Without a system of cognitive structures defined and shared by their group, parents probably would not have acquired enough knowledge to do what was necessary to nurture children until they were able to fend for themselves. The species would have disappeared, for this ability to program minds in shared and cumulative ways, rather than trust to mere instinct, is the human's means of survival. In sum, the human mind becomes a *cognitive system*, that is, a framework of mental constructs of the external world and of beliefs, images, assumptions, habits of reasoning, etc., by which the continuing barrage of stimuli a person receives can be sorted out and given meaning. Even beliefs that do not have a basis in reality can be useful in this regard. Whether they are fully accurate or not, stereotypes too have a function, providing a way to make sense of one's environment with the speed necessary to produce a response when urgently needed. It is within this psychological reality that we must, in the final analysis, expect to manage our international problem-solving. These processes are not subject to fundamental change.

If one's overall cognitive system is to serve its purpose, it must have a substantial degree of stability over time. Its component elements have to be mutually compatible, at least in large degree, and it has to be enough in tune with the real world and with the cognitive systems of other people to allow the individual to meet basic physical and social needs. Hence, to keep things tidy and consistent:

a. *We perceive very selectively in accordance with the structure of cognitive systems,* as will be discussed further below. It would be inefficient, even counterproductive, to notice everything there is to notice, so our cognitive system allows us to perceive selectively without conscious effort, without having to decide in each case. Thus, a casual American newspaper reader might come to a page with, among other items, two stories with equally prominent headlines. One is headed "Attempt to Hijack American Aircraft Foiled by Alert Security Guard," and another headed "Government of Country X Resigns After Parliament Votes No Confidence." The reader may notice and read the first, then go on to the next page without even seeing the second item or any others on the page. It is not a matter of which is actually the more important, but what the reader is tuned by experience and interest to notice.

b. *We tend to perceive in a way that will disturb our established cognitive system as little as possible* and to interpret what we perceive in a manner consistent with our own particular mindset. We do not easily accommodate discordant facts if our cognitive systems are doing the jobs they are supposed to. Thus, while the news item above might identify the hijacker as, let us say, a distraught rejected lover, the average reader would probably conclude simply that terrorists are striking again. A teenager or a more intensely romantic person might, on the other hand, perceive the event as a vivid life drama with no relation to international politics.

This is not to say that cognitive systems never change. However, in changing, the mind still seeks consistency. Its changes are made up of ongoing adjustments. When the parts do lose their internal consistency , or new information or experience cannot be interpreted satisfactorily—when there is *cognitive dissonance,* to use standard terminology—the chance for seeking alternative explanations is greatest. Ironically, a mind at peace is a mind that is closed.

2. *The way we perceive is much more locked in than we realize.* In perceiving the world and what happens in it, we think that we are in charge. Sometimes we are, but the evidence indicates that our internal computers are rather rigidly programmed as to what incoming data will be accepted and how it will be processed. It takes considerable effort to override our habitual ways of perceiving and reasoning, to break out of established mindsets. We (our conscious selves) are thus not so much in charge as we think.

The reason for this is that what we end up perceiving is actually much more than "meets the eye." That is, most perception starts with some kind of limited stimulus that, in effect, triggers a release of previous experience to round out the whole picture. The stimulus may be a word, a symbol, a picture, a scene from one vantage point, but rarely will a stimulus carry so complete a meaning as to be sufficient in itself. The mind must still add pieces to complete the picture.

Hence, we can say that people are very selective in what they perceive directly through their senses. Then, what is perceived through the senses is enlarged upon as the incoming data is entered into the existing cognitive system and assigned its meaning. Consequently, for better or worse, we can perceive the item or event without necessarily seeing the whole; or we can perceive what is probably there, or, by a misfiring of the trigger process, perceive that which is not there at all! Thus the potential for *misperception.*

This leap from stimulus to a fuller blown idea is amply demonstrated in the process of visual perception. In a civilization where we are surrounded by right angles in windows and walls and a multitude of daily objects, we expect to "see" rectangles where rectangles are supposed to be. Thus, if asked about the shape of a desk top or table in a room, one would not hesitate to report that it is rectangular; a group of people looking at the same desk top would also agree. Yet it would be highly unlikely any of the observers would be looking at the desk from directly above or below it, the only angles where an image of a perfect rectangle can be projected onto the retina of the eye. Thus, no one present actually physically observes a rectangle where they perceive one. What happens is that each pair of eyes in the assembled group picks up stimuli that fit into what is *already* known about tables, desks, windows and room corners, and the computer banks of the several minds present supply *something in addition* to what is actually received through the senses. The importance of the "something supplied in addition" can hardly be overestimated in our discussion of the effect of mindsets, of course.

As psychologists can demonstrate, this additional input can be so strong that it becomes very difficult to perceive variations from what is expected because they would conflict with the cognitive system as established. This is the basis for optical illusions.

The classic example is the experimental distorted room developed by Hadley Cantril and colleagues in their Princeton research facilities. A full-sized room is constructed, but the floor and ceiling are not level, the windows are not quite rectangular and corners are distorted. All this is done so cleverly that from a certain observation point at one end of the room, all appears normally proportioned. Then, in experiments, identical objects—even people—are placed in the corners of the room. But instead of causing us as observers to see that the room is in fact distorted, our perceptions are adjusted to fit our belief in the normality of the room. We perceive the two identical objects as being different sizes, one large and one small. When the objects are reversed in position, they grow or shrink accordingly. Interestingly, even when the observer knows intellectually the true nature of the room or has even been allowed to enter and examine it, it is still nearly impossible to perceive the sizes of the objects correctly—impossible, in other words, to visually perceive reality as it is. What one's cognitive system imposes on one's visual perception is too strong.[3] (Note that while the kind of perceptual breakdown illustrated by this experiment is dysfunctional, most of the time it is handy indeed not to have to get oneself into a position to see desk tops or rooms in full rectangular display in order to be able to judge the shape!)

The reader is familiar enough with optical illusions and needs only extend the example a little to see that the same process is at work when a foreign mindset, suspicious of U.S. intentions, leads its owner to "see" a CIA agent in a Peace Corps volunteer, or leads a thoroughly programmed mind such as that of the late Secretary of State, John Foster Dulles, to "see" only Communist machinations behind every overseas disturbance.

Moving from psychology to social psychology carries our examination of this subject to its next level of complexity—that of programmed perception and reasoning as a function of interaction with other people. One's cognitive system is molded by society and culture, by education and the socialization process, social experience, information and knowledge transmitted from other people, and, in specific situations, by suggestion and a sense of group sanction or censure. Through social experience, habits of perceiving and reasoning become, in large degree, those of the groups to which we as individuals belong. Such commonality provides the shared outlooks that make social life possible. We will examine this subject in greater detail in the next chapter, as it is crucial to understanding how *patterns* of perception and reasoning differ across cultures. But for the moment, the point is that the way a person perceives other people, interprets what they are doing and why, and chooses how to respond to them, is also locked in by sociocultural circumstances. This phenomenon eventually extends to the way one society perceives another.

Social psychologists spend much of their waking hours studying regularities in the social perception process, and their introductory texts are concerned with the effects of stereotyping, interpersonal perceptions, attitudes and attitude change, persuasion, and much more that need not be repeated here. But their study and their experimental evidence all support the idea that in social as in physical reality, people perceive, reason, and respond not necessarily according to the facts, but *according to the image they have of the facts.* They also stress that social images or mindsets regarding people, as in the case of rectangles and optical illusions, tend to purposefully channel the range of perception alternatives, generally making it highly improbable that one can override all one's mental habits in the interest of objectivity. Thus, as in our interactions with the physical world, we have developed social "optical illusions" in interacting with people—and probably with much greater frequency.

One further facet of the locked-in perception phenomenon needs to be considered at this point. The more abstract the subject to be perceived—a point of law, a development plan, a religious tenet, a work of art—the more one will necessarily draw on the resources of the cognitive system to establish substance and meaning. That is, in constructing a picture of an intangible issue, the proportion of information that comes from previous experience and knowledge (in contrast to that which is available from the actual stimulus) is going to be higher than if the subject were more concrete. While you may "see" a production plan, for example, as words or flow charts on paper, you cannot actually "see" it until it is executed, and then probably not as one entity.

Hence, the potential for variation in the way that abstract subjects are perceived and reasoned about is very substantial, especially when perceptions are made from the vantage points of differing societies or positions within societies. And in international professional-level activities, abstract subjects are of constant concern. For example, the following are all very abstract concepts as far as our perception of them is concerned: capitalism, political ideologies, contractual obligations, cultural exchange, educational philosophy or advertising appeals. But the psychological principle still applies, even more so. Perception and reasoning are programmed, even locked in, unless a very concerted intellectual effort is made to open up the process.

Or, turned the other way around, perceiving abstract subjects *requires* the help of a supporting cognitive system. If the subject that is called to one's attention is entirely "foreign," that is, completely outside one's experience, it will be difficult to assign even a distorted meaning to it. An example for Westerners might be Buddhist theology. Even when explained repeatedly, it resists comprehension by Westerners, who have to acquire a complex new frame of reference in order to understand it. For most, the same would apply to the theory of relativity. The appropriate "software" for one's mental computer is missing. In these cases, perception is "locked out" rather than locked in.

It is apparent that in seeking an applied social psychology for international practice, the objective often will be to capture a workable understanding of the *various* cognitive systems—of individuals or of groups—that may come into play relative to a given issue or problem. Later we will propose a check list for exploring mindsets, and much of this book will be directed toward sharpening one's ability to anticipate contrasting outlooks.

3. *There are fewer universal commonalities in human thought processes than most people think.* One of the threads that will run

through our argument will be the need to be wary of those who claim universality for certain beliefs or for particular ways human beings think or express emotion. While all human beings are essentially alike in physical composition, share certain fundamental needs and potentials, and are sentimentally "brothers under the skin," the supposed commonalities of "human nature" prove evanescent where mindsets and perception habits are concerned. In fact, the range of what can be considered normal across cultures is very broad. Even what might be defined as needing psychiatric help in one society may be considered quite sane in another. Culture and personality studies conducted by anthropologists have documented stark contrasts in the most fundamental aspects of human existence: cosmology, ethics, meaning of death, family roles, governance.

These kinds of contrasts were highlighted during World War II when Americans, in an effort to predict Japanese actions, were brought face to face with, to them, incomprehensible behaviors: suicide bombing, for instance, or unexpectedly cooperative prisoner behavior immediately after what was considered by Americans to be irrational attempts to avoid capture—including suicide. Twenty-eight years after the war ended, one Lieutenant Onoda gained international attention when he was discovered still hiding out on Lubang Island in the Philippines. He had never surrendered; he had never been ordered to do so and had spent all those years honorably surviving in the Philippine jungle until a change in his duty was defined by acceptable authority. After his eventual return to Japan, there was a wave of approbation for his exemplary behavior and the degree to which it accorded with Japanese values, although some thought it a bit overdone.[1]

The importance of this kind of radical variation in values and behavior can hardly be overstated. After all, it is the enduring mindsets of both the general public and their leaders—exemplified in the extreme by Lt. Onoda—that plague our efforts to find solutions to the highest orders of world problems.

4. *How one perceives events, issues or policies depends on how they are presented.* While much of the emphasis in this book will be placed on how contrasting mindsets channel perceptions, perception also depends on the way that subject matter is presented. Psychologists stress the need to study the nature of the stimulus. This is also the

concern of artists, advertisers, propagandists, and psychological warfare specialists, all of whom are practicing applied psychology in their specialized fields. Again, there are basics to consider. Stimuli can vary in intensity, in strength, in duration and repetition, and in the way they are tuned to fit into the needs and interests of the perceiver.

Perhaps the most important consideration for foreign affairs applications is that perception is affected by the context in which a specific stimulus is presented, and by the way that the context itself is perceived and understood. A military exercise may be perceived as threatening or defensive, depending on what else is going on at the same time. For example, the continuing state of tension between the U.S. and the USSR supplies the context for interpreting almost any action or statement by the other as a devious plot or aggressive strategy.

International news stories carried on evening television may be interpreted in entirely different ways, depending on contextual factors that affect perception—what else is going on at the time, whether the story is placed at the beginning or end of the program, how dramatic the film footage is, what tone of voice the reporter uses. Conversely, meaning can be changed by leaving out the context. A street demonstration photographed by a narrow-angle lens to cut out the bemused and peaceful onlookers may appear far more significant to the TV viewer than to someone at the scene.

In conducting many routine international activities, this context effect has to be taken into account in reverse. That is, when abroad, your own words or actions are held captive to the way your presence, mission, nationality or apparent social position is perceived and understood by your hosts, for this sets the stage for interpreting what you are saying and doing. There may not be much you can do about it, but the accuracy of a counterpart's perception might be enhanced by adding background explanation, carefully timing your presentation, selecting the best setting or situation, and adding to your team local personnel who understand your position and intentions. You are well advised, therefore, to try to anticipate a counterpart's sense of context if you wish to manage an accurate and favorable reception to your action or message. Accomplishing this, unfortunately, is complicated by the point discussed next.

5. *The naive but normal practice is to project one's own mindset onto other people.* "That price is outrageous and they know it." "The contract is specific, so the Japanese cannot expect us to review the problem yet again." This is a common kind of reaction. If I see something in a given way, others must see it that way too. Even more, the normal and unconscious assumption is that the habitual ways of thinking of one's own society are a matter of human nature and therefore have universal application.

There is much to be gained by the direct application to foreign affairs of "projection theory." For example, Marc Lewis reported a tendency to project in Central Intelligence Agency estimates in Vietnam. He found that American analysts interpreted developments there by projecting much more of an American frame of reference onto events than they were aware of. This led to seriously distorted interpretations when they tried to explain and predict political developments in a foreign and very different Vietnamese society and culture.[5]

Congressman Les Aspin suggested somewhat the same thing in an article in *Foreign Policy*.[6] He noted that distortions may have been introduced in U.S. intelligence estimates of Soviet military threats because analysts tended to focus mainly on hard evidence of technical capabilities rather than on intentions or Soviet conceptions of how hardware would be used—that is, on knowing "what is going on inside Soviet heads." He argued that Americans see mirror images in judging future Soviet offensive capabilities by projecting onto the Soviets their own assumptions as to how resources, including nuclear weapons, will be deployed and used.

This tendency to project is normal for people in any society, of course, for culture's function is to establish a more or less homogeneous set of beliefs and assumptions by which everyone can project their perception expectations onto other people without thinking about it. This provides the sense of security that comes with predictability; it is the cement that holds societies together; it vastly simplifies interaction and cooperation. At home it is best if everyone does internalize the society's common sense beliefs and attitudes, even though they inevitably mistake them for "human nature." But when interaction crosses national lines, naive projection is not supportable. Therefore, judgments are often off the mark and responses become unpredictable.

This problem is a continuing one for the United States Information Agency and the Voice of America, whose task it is to explain to the world the nature of American society and the intent of U.S. policies and actions in world affairs. In Washington USIA administrators tend to project what they have learned about communication at home when directing operations and preparing programs and materials for foreign audiences. Accordingly, they are prone to use the kind of people, methods and procedures found successful in American advertising, and, for efficiency, they develop standard packages of information to be used in all countries with, at most, the translation required to adapt it to specific language "targets." Overseas, more experienced career professionals are in a constant state of frustration. They know international communication does not work that way. They want materials designed to communicate a message in their particular country of assignment, one that takes into account the way that their audience will actually see and comprehend what USIA is trying to say.

With USIA's predilection to focus first on the communication equipment and program design that will "reach" the audience, the assumption is too easily made that one will know automatically what to tell or show an audience once it is reached. The result is programs aimed at a high tech projection of American mindsets rather than programs designed to communicate with mindsets that in almost all cases will impose at least some variation of meaning on the information transmitted, however fast or sophisticated the method.

Try to explain in China, Pakistan or the Soviet Union, for example, the virtues of volunteer organizations such as the League of Women Voters or the Society for the Prevention of Cruelty to Animals. The rationale for these organizations and their missions, which seems to Americans too obvious to mention, will almost never project completely accurately onto a foreign audience. Many intended messages thus become unguided missiles when judged in terms of how they are actually understood. When USIA has to explain fast-moving U.S. actions, it has an even greater problem. Sample: The U.S. aids the El Salvadoran government in fighting off an insurgency while in Nicaragua it aids the insurgents to fight off the government. Try to explain to audiences looking on from afar why all this makes sense to Americans in the first place, and why it should make sense to *them* in the second. The answer that, in effect, too often comes back from USIA is: if it makes sense to us, it *ought* to make sense to other people. Of course, if a policy produces "cognitive dissonance" for Americans too, USIA is especially hard pressed!

6. *Attribution of motive is a form of projection that is particularly important in foreign affairs.* This is a spin-off from attribution theory in social psychology. The idea is that in order to interpret what people are doing, we normally and consistently *attribute motives* to them, and usually do so unconsciously. The motives attributed are those common to one's experience as related to the situation of the moment, the category of person, and the expected role.

The following is an illustration. In one of my early ventures abroad I was part of a group of American students working as volunteers in public health projects in rural Mexico, rather like the later Peace Corps. We did a lot of physical labor, especially digging drainage ditches and pits for latrines, as part of an effort to control malaria and improve sanitation. To the local community we explained our volunteer work in terms of working for better international understanding, of humanitarian service, and of any number of other cliches that go with "doing good." All this was rather far removed from local experience, and people were not convinced. Instead, they attributed motives to us that did make sense based on their experience with foreigners and strangers: we were looking for oil or digging for gold. Perhaps the "attribution of motive" that satisfied them most was that we were doing penance!

This kind of experience is familiar to those who have lived abroad; it seems that others are constantly misattributing motives to us, either naively or perversely. What we fail to see is that we too misattribute motives. Combine the error on both sides and it can be argued that nothing obstructs international interchange as much as this psychological mechanism running amok in a cross-cultural situation. Misattributing motives and intentions is a central thread that potentially runs through all international relations calculations, from those made by policy makers to those propounded by self-styled experts in the neighborhood bar. And the most intractable misattributions are the products of mindsets of which the actors are unaware; they may even fail to perceive subsequent evidence that motives have been misattributed.

One of the more dramatic cases occurred when a Soviet fighter plane shot down Korean Airlines Flight 007, an unarmed passenger jet, in Soviet air space over a sensitive area near Sakhalin Island in 1983. Americans, with the President and the press in the lead, immediately attributed the motive to a trigger-happy and callous Soviet disregard for human life, assuming that the action was taken with full knowledge that the plane being attacked was a passenger aircraft. As it turned out, according to later analysis, this was not quite what happened. When the Korean aircraft strayed from its flight path, the Soviets also misattributed motives. In fact, the pilot who downed the passenger plane apparently never imagined that it was not a foreign reconnaissance military plane. The attack might later still be interpreted as a trigger-happy response, even by the Soviets themselves, but the point is that the damage was compounded and decision making confused by this form of jumping to conclusions.

Even when conscious attempts are made to be objective in examining intentions, as in the analytical work that goes into strategy formulation or institutional decision making, the analysis can still be flawed by misprojecting motives. It has been suggested that those who have conducted scholarly and supposedly objective analyses of Soviet affairs in the postwar years might have been victims of a kind of "group think" that needs reconsideration. Stephen Cohen, in his book *Rethinking the Soviet Experience: Politics and History Since 1917,*[7] argues that the cold war mentality led to a certain conventional wisdom regarding the motives of the Soviets. That mentality has become something of a boiler plate explanation of Communist behavior, dulling the standard scientific inquiry: "What else is true: how otherwise can one explain the phenomena under study?" In effect, analysts, who otherwise pride themselves on their independent judgment, are bound in some degree to a collective mindset.

In his *Fearful Warriors: A Psychological Profile of U.S.-Soviet Relations,*[8] Ralph White argues forcefully that in analyzing Russian intentions, one must find the means to *empathize* with their perception of issues and events, even though one is not prepared to *sympathize* with them. History as seen through their eyes, he suggests, is dominated by a vast scene of destruction which occurred on their own soil during World War II. Therefore, they can be expected to be hypersensitive regarding the prospect of any renewed violation of their borders. Add to this their particular sense of their own internal objectives and problems and one already has a good part of an explanation for their confrontation with the West, an explanation that may well differ from the motives attributed to them as a projection of images held in the U.S. Understanding Soviet motives in this way may not make the Russians any less threatening, but it provides a much better basis for selecting our initiatives and calculating our responses.

7. *Institutionalized information processing is also a study in perception and reasoning.* A predominant part of international activity revolves around formally, and even scientifically, processing information in institutional settings—selecting, storing, recalling, and transmitting it, and using it in solving problems. Increasingly, we refer to some of the technologically advanced countries as "information societies" because producing and using information tends to surpass agriculture or industrial production as mainstream activities. It follows that international society itself is also based to an ever larger extent on the flow and use of information, most especially news flow. Therefore, along with the level of individual perception and reasoning, the psychology of information processing in more institutional contexts becomes an important consideration.

When we think of handling information, we tend to assume a distinctly rational or objective level of mental activity by educated and experienced people. There is a tendency to expect that formal information processing will be carried out above the level of mindset complications, that all educated people would be led by the same information and evidence to the same conclusions, more or less as Aristotle argued. Yet, for the purposes of our discussion here, the question still persists: how subjective is this process? Is it a function of all the perception and reasoning factors set forth above, or can people exercise authority over the psychological forces that distort reality and thereby take control of the information processing that is required of humans as problemsolvers and shapers of their own environment?

This question goes quickly to the heart of the philosophy of scientific methodology. In fact, psychological theory does see human thinking as being far from passive in its decision-making mode.[9] Even in pursuing the subject matter of this book, our attempt to "think about thought" represents a mental activity of a high order. Yet, both cross-cultural evidence and the problems encountered in the pursuit of true scientific objectivity indicate that a full escape from subjectivity is rare if not nonexistent. Values, implicit assumptions that are not easily recognized and controlled, styles of reasoning, possibly an epistomology that is tied to language and its structure, all stand out as the uncontrolled variables in information processing. In any case, most of the time in international relations activities, people are at best amateur scientists in their quest for gaining and using information, sifting evidence, and relating cause and effect. Adding research staffs and computer technology does not *necessarily* improve the quality of information processing, although such does add to a capacity for it.

Part of the difficulty, psychologists warn, is that in institutions information is produced and used in group settings, that is, in the context of group processes and collective decision making in staff meetings, through multiple copies of interoffice memos, in board reviews, sign-off procedures, interagency or interdepartmental panels, and a maze of informal consulting. This tends to fortify the effect of conventional wisdom and the subjective meaning and interpretation that goes with the group's larger social experience and intellectual moorings. In other words, the group setting draws the net of culture or subculture tighter and restrains such individual creativity as might conflict with the larger prescriptions of the society. The interaction in such information processing and decision making brings into play the psychological principles of group dynamics. As noted earlier, Irving Janis has produced a clear reminder of this in his book *Victims of Group Think*.[10] In it he examines the ways in which conflicting interpretations of information are compromised, how subjective common sense is reinforced, and how even conclusions that individual members of the group might doubt if working alone are reinforced by group consensus. We also noted that Alexander George, in his *Presidential Decision Making in Foreign Policy*, has made an extensive study of the way this process operates in the U.S. executive branch of the government.[11]

The psychologists' counsel, then, is that quality can be achieved in information processing and decision making only by confronting this situational potential for misperception which fortifies subjective and erroneous interpretations. Methods have to be adopted by decision makers which enable them to review context, develop alternative explanations, and uncover the patterns of belief by which naive diagnoses are made. This is especially needed when decision makers are fatigued or under stress, or are working under severe time constraints.

The "group think" problem is particularly apropos in examining the decision-making process in international affairs, for each national group involved has to be able to consider in some detail the lens through which its own culture views the world. As the preceding discussion should make clear, decision makers are not easily prepared to do so.

8. *Language differences are more significant as factors in perception and reasoning than one expects.* As noted at the beginning of the chapter, the words we use to express ideas and communicate experience are themselves ways of categorizing and simplifying the environment, ways of helping the mind get organized.

The importance of this point in practical application needs emphasis. Words can become, in effect, minimindsets. As we know from the study of semantics, by choosing one word over another we supply different programming for treating the subject at hand. When a press report chooses between "terrorists" and "freedom fighters," the perception and reasoning that follow have been channeled at the outset. This is why official announcements and news reports are so important and can have such an impact. Whatever the subject, the writer has the opportunity to code the action, to choose the category to be used in thinking about it, and to predispose listeners or readers to desired conclusions. Alternative conclusions can also be cut off. Hence, a bank loan in default looks better from the start if it is labeled a "non-performing" loan. Civilians killed in a bombing raid are not anyone's responsibility, really; they are part of "collateral damage." Political leaders do not lie, they "misspeak." A strategist does not take a gamble, but a "calculated risk." Our community does not have a garbage dump, but a "landfill."

All this has significance enough for understanding perception and reasoning when just one language is involved. The question raised in going from one language to another is whether words used in translation bring to bear equivalent minimindsets. The question becomes even more important when abstract ideas are concerned. Consider concepts like capitalism, socialism, public interest, corporate responsibility, human rights. *Complete* translation into other languages is unlikely when the problem of equating the minimindsets that go with the words is taken into account, as will be more apparent in light of the effects of culture treated in the next chapter. However, we should point out here that if a minimindset exists for speakers of one language and not another, the problem cannot be met by ordinary translation. One of my favorite examples is the outlook on life and on relations among people that we incorporate into the term "fair play." I invite the reader to try translating this—both the word and the minimindset that goes with it—into any language of choice.

This raises the further question of what happens in the conduct of international business when translation and interpretation are used, or when one side is speaking in a second language. How much does one switch from one pattern of perceiving and reasoning to another when speaking a foreign language? Language and culture are so closely related that an answer to this will require thinking through the effect of culture on language, as we will do in the next chapter.

But there is another aspect of language, perception and reasoning which, according to specialists in psycho-cultural studies, causes even more difficulties in international communications. They argue that beyond words and choice of phrases, the basic grammar and fundamental structure of a language presents a model or master framework for channeling cognitive processes, for conceptualizing the environment and the manner in which its elements interrelate, and for choosing the way that one idea leads to the next. In short, is one likely to think the same way in all languages? Benjamin Lee Whorf thought not. His "Whorfian hypothesis" proposed that "the structure of the language one habitually uses influences the manner in which one understands his environment;" that is, "the picture of the universe shifts from tongue to tongue." Whorf argued that "we are thus introduced to a new principle of relativity, which holds that all observers are not led by the same physical evidence to the same picture of the universe, unless their linguistic backgrounds are similar, or can in some way be calibrated."[12]

While the Whorfian hypothesis is disputed by many linguists, it is nevertheless highly suggestive for the analysis of cross-cultural interaction. If different languages represent differing psychological worlds, people working internationally have to wonder if their own thoughts and usual patterns of reasoning are really striking responsive chords in the thinking of speakers of another language. While the hypothesis may not be particularly useful when language structures are relatively similar, as in the case of European languages, anthropologists tend to line up with Whorf when the contrasts are across language families—English and Chinese, for example, or English and Arabic.

Fuller exploration of Whorfian theory is beyond the scope of this book. However, when you notice an interpreter using consecutive rather than simultaneous interpretation, be alert! Someone is having trouble squeezing the logic of the message through the interpreting mill. When we say that "it loses something in translation," finding out what that "something" is may be the most important element in bridging mindsets.

The ideas discussed in this chapter, taken from psychological theory and research, are somewhat arbitrarily chosen, but they can serve as starters in looking at the role mindsets play in everyday international activities. The next step will be to explore the connection between culture and mindsets, a step not taken frequently enough when the psychological dimension of international relations is analyzed.

CHAPTER THREE

The Cultural Lens

Working in international relations is a special endeavor because one has to deal with entirely new patterns of mindsets. To the extent that they can be identified and anticipated for particular groups or even nations, some of the mystery inherent in the conduct of "foreign" affairs will diminish. Thus the concern of this chapter: the role that culture and national experience play in producing predictable mindsets.

Here are a few examples where contrasting *patterns of thinking* make the difference in international behavior. In 1982 the British, and many others, were surprised when Argentina took military action to occupy the Falkland Islands, or Malvinas, as Argentines call the islands. This set off a short but intense war that appeared to have insufficient cause and, as it turned out, disastrous consequences for Argentina. Part of the surprise was the very idea that Argentines could become that agitated about a sovereignty issue that de facto had been "settled" a hundred and fifty years before, or over real estate that was so dubious an asset. The British and Americans were inclined to think of the past as past: Argentine claims, even if they had some validity, had no practical importance in the late twentieth century. But it became dramatically evident that the Argentines viewed "the past" *per se* through other lenses and that this past was vividly alive in the collective Argentine mind. Combined with other concerns and preoccupations, their sense of history was strong enough to make a military option seem reasonable. In projecting their own sense of the reasonableness of their cause, they erroneously expected world opinion to understand and support them. Instead, much of the world, especially the British and Americans, found the action somewhat preposterous, even comic, had it not been so deadly. Yet the war was on. At the very least, two sharply contrasting ways of thinking about the significance of historical events were in play. Clearly, people who share a common culture or national experience do tend to react to events in similar ways and reflect common mindsets that allow observers to speak of national or cultural characteristics, as "Argentine" or "British" modes of response, for instance.

Watergate is another example. While the scandal was unfolding in the United States, the French had something of a collective difficulty in understanding what the fuss was all about, or at least the extent of the fuss. They could not empathize with the sense of moral outrage that prompted the American people to drive a president from office. The acts that Americans defined as unethical or as an abuse of power were not seen by the French in as sharp an ethical relief. They would not have given it the political or moral priority Americans did. Similarly, the French tend to find American insistence on the moral correctness of many of their positions in world affairs rather unconvincing. They see a big power acting like a big power, and moral explanations seem to be unnecessary rationalizations.[1]

Other contrasts in American and French patterns of assumptions and reasoning could be noted. It has been observed by those involved that on entering into negotiation the American assumption is that the negotiating partner can be trusted until proven otherwise; the French, on the other hand, tend to mistrust the other until a basis for trust has been established. In arguing cases in negotiation, the French prefer a style of presentation by which one moves from point to point in a kind of deductive Cartesian logic, while Americans tend to argue their cause on inductive evidence and pragmatic application to the problem. Also, the French prefer to take a longer range view of problems and their solutions, Americans a more immediate one, or as was said of a U.S. policy maker, "He does not look very far over the horizon." Thus, in conducting American-French business, a difference in cognitive patterns and style must be bridged along with any difference in substantive positions.[2]

In all of these instances, psychological factors are involved, but the nature of that psychology is a function of the particular national culture. This leads to renewed consideration of the studies in culture and personality that cultural anthropologists have pursued over recent decades, for the internationalist's task is to take the next critical step in applying concepts from social psychology: introduce into the equation the way that national societies and cultures produce their own brands of cognition. This relationship between culture and mindset comprises the fundamental variable in international dialogue. While people differ in their individual ways of thinking, their differences become variations on basic themes supplied by the culture.

This means that people look on international issues and events through a *cultural lens*. Again, we may be using a term that is more popular than technical, but "cultural lens" does focus attention on the connection between culture and personality, and therefore on the connection between culture and general regularities in cultural conditioning as far as perceiving and reasoning are concerned. It is the lens, ground and colored according to the prescription of a culture or to the cultural conditioning derived therefrom, through which everyone who has experienced that particular kind of conditioning views the world. This is not quite the same as mindset; the cultural lens is a more fundamental aspect of thinking and perceiving, the basic resource programming from which mindsets are, in part, drawn and with which they tend to be consistent. Thus, the use of the word "lens" should not be taken too literally, since culture is a basic determinant of mindsets, not simply a filter for them. A mindset, on the other hand, designates a more narrowly focused or discreet way of thinking or perceiving that will reflect culture's conditioning, but might also reflect other sources of mental programming that would not be included in the usual meaning of culture.

So, this chapter explores the press of culture and urges that we turn our usual approach around and look first to group-shared inclinations to perceive and reason in given ways. It is the general practice in making psychological estimates in international affairs to start with individual decisionmakers at the center of attention and then extend the analysis of their decisions to the effect of surrounding rings of contributing factors—the influence of advisors, inner workings of institutions, the thinking of pertinent elites, public opinion and political processes. Culture tends to be considered last, as having only a broad or diffuse impact on ways of perceiving and reasoning, or, more frequently, it is left out altogether. Hence, even when the approach includes an exploration of psychological factors, it ends up, at least to some degree, being ethnocentric.

For example, in his ambitious *Perception and Misperception in International Politics*,[3] previously cited, Robert Jervis simply tells the reader that he has chosen not to pursue cross-cultural aspects of the subject. In the summary review of international decisionmaking, *Structure of Decision*, edited by Robert Axelrod,[4] cultural factors receive only passing mention in a few paragraphs. In all the research on "operational codes"—otherwise a particularly useful conceptual approach—the cultural dimension receives little explicit treatment. This is also true for cognitive mapping.[5] The implication is that there is some fundamental international universality in the decision-making process, the dynamics of which can be understood by seeking out selected universally applicable psychological variables.

When our concern is *international* interaction, failing to consider how psychological factors vary with culture is poor science to start with, and exceptionally bad applied science. Consequently, we will first examine how people start out being alike within their own culture. For this, a brief refresher on the culture concept might be useful.

THE CULTURE CONCEPT

Just what does "culture" mean? It is a term used both technically and in everyday speech, so the chances are that unless the reader has had occasion to be precise about it, the implications of what we have to say about the cultural dimension may be only superficially appreciated.

Let us start by cutting out some of the brush. In some usages, culture equates with civilization and its products. Thus, one is exploring Greek culture in visiting the Parthenon, or British culture in touring the theater district or the Houses of Parliament. Fair enough, but that does not suit our purposes. Another way of thinking about culture is embodied in the phrase "a cultured person": someone who behaves urbanely, has a taste for gourmet foods and uses the proper utensils to eat them, carries on serious conversations about the arts, and is not given to rude displays of temper. Again, put that aside for our purposes here.

Getting more anthropological, culture often means customs, that is, traditional or characteristic activities that can be observed, such as tribal dances, religious rites, marriage practices, etc. To add confusion, this way of looking at culture also often includes artifacts: canoe paddles, masks, or arrowheads, which we put in museums. Further, culture tends to be considered as something to describe the ways of primitive tribes but not those of modern and sophisticated people with lots of college degrees. Finally, confusion is compounded when culture comes to mean the people themselves, so we speak of the Masai people or the Chinese as a "culture"—something like the organisms to be seen on a laboratory slide. Actually, people make up a *society*, which in turn *has* a culture.

A proper definition of culture depends, of course, on who is using the word and in what context. But as a *culture concept* has come to be meaningful in the context of the behavioral sciences, the emphasis has shifted away from attempting a one-line definition to calling attention to a *set of implications* that derive from culture's function as the human being's unique way of coping with the environment (both physical and social) and surviving.

Perhaps the easiest way to appreciate the culture concept is to consider the newborn child. It enters the world quite inadequately equipped to cope with all the problems it will face in getting food and shelter, combating disease, avoiding harm, associating with other humans, and making sense of all the experiences that will be its human lot —from understanding why thunderstorms come along to comprehending the meaning of death. The child will not be able to depend simply on instinct. On the other hand, it will have some extraordinary assets: a brain potential that is still unthreatened by the most sophisticated computers, an ability to use speech, a prehensile hand, and considerable physical adaptability—just think of the variety of food sources that humans around the world can use. In other words, the infant mind is somewhat like a blank tape, waiting to be filled, and culture plays a large part in the recording process.

Culture is a pretested *design*, a store of knowledge and an entire system of coping skills that has been crafted by humans who have gone before, a design that has been socially created, tested and shared, and one that can be transmitted to the child. It is this design, which persists even as individuals come and go, that makes all the difference for humans. So culture is *learned* behavior, although the learning is often out of awareness. It is *shared* behavior, which is important because it systematizes the way people do things, thus avoiding confusion and allowing cooperation so that groups of people can accomplish what no single individual could alone. And it is behavior that is imposed by sanctions, rewards and punishments for those who are part of the group.

What are some of the important implications? One is that if humans can develop one set of customs, they can also develop other sets. They thus can adapt to a wide range of circumstances, with cultures differing accordingly. Consequently, culture is variable; there is no one universally preferred or "natural" way of life, and standards for evaluating cultures must, to a large extent, be comparative and relative. What is appropriate in the desert might not work in New York.

A second implication is that culture is organized. The parts fit together. A custom accordingly makes sense only in relation to the larger system, the overall culture of which it is a part. Taking customary behaviors out of their cultural contexts and judging them within another makes them almost impossible to understand.

A third implication, and one especially important for our purposes, is that if culture is learned and internalized, it can be considered "customs-of-the-mind," or a system of customs-of-the-mind. It prepares one to think like other people in the group think, to perceive and reason in ways that will predispose them to behavior which fits into the society's mold. It follows that for internationalists, the area of cultural anthropology in which the connection between culture and personality is studied becomes the most fascinating.

Note how it works. In the process of absorbing my own culture, I, like those around me, come to understand that atoms exist even though I have never seen one, that policemen are to be respected, that cheating is wrong in most situations, that dogs should be petted and not eaten, and that an eight-tone scale makes pleasant music. In my smaller and more specialized social groups, I might have some more specialized customs-of-the-mind; in a graduate school, I come to expect that a grade of "C" means trouble, or in my scientifically oriented culture, I come to reason in terms of cause and effect.

Whatever my culture, I might get away with some individual variations in what I think and believe, but I cannot wander too far from the path of my group's pattern of thinking and get along. In this regard, I have always liked the explanation for the difference between the psychotic and the neurotic. The psychotic believes that two and two are five—he has wandered off the path. The neurotic agrees that two and two are four but worries about it!

In sum the culture concept allows us to think of culture in terms of psychological behavior, and there is much to be gained by that. Let us suggest, for there is no precise way to calculate such things, that 80% of the explanation for a person's acquired behavior is to be found in the cultural patterns imposed by that person's social group and normally absorbed and internalized without much effort. The remaining 20% fits into the category of the uniquely individual. If this is a reasonable estimate—even while recognizing that the percentages will vary according to a culture's homogeneity and rigidness—then the most efficient way to understand differences in international behavior will be to look for significant differences in mindsets imposed by the culture, in the standard operating procedures which define the way individuals in the group are expected to perceive and reason about the world around them.

THE COMPUTER PROGRAMMING ANALOGY APPLIED TO COMMUNICATION

Perhaps suggesting that human minds are programmed like computers is questionable as scientific procedure; the analogy may be too facile. Even though the computer seems overpoweringly mysterious to the noninitiated—a mass of ingeniously interconnected silicon chips containing almost microscopic integrated circuits—human cerebral physiology is considerably more complicated and mysterious. Still, the comparison may serve a useful heuristic purpose in analyzing communication across cultures, for we are saying that culture supplies the master programming, or the basic software, for perceiving and reasoning.

Certainly the human cognitive system does have a formidable range of function. Not only can past events persist in memory, but even in a kind of collective memory that is transmitted from a previous generation—the essence of culture. Future events can exist in expectations, along with purely imaginary events in daydreams. We can experience vicariously and add to our psychological worlds the vast variety of other people's experiences through the symbolism of written and spoken words. We can deal in abstractions. We can think up new things or events and even communicate them to the psychological worlds of other people without any evidence that they ever did or will exist in the world of reality. And we can capture otherwise hidden realities through theory and inference, as in the case of atomic physics.

However, note that in most discussion of international communication, the larger part of analytic effort simply goes into describing factors *external* to what is going on in our minds; that is, the focus is on the situation, the events and issues themselves, and interplay of the "actors." The programmed minds that process the factors are taken for granted. Most international news coverage, for example, reports observable events and selected supporting facts, but tends to leave out the special meaning the events have for those involved in that place and culture. It also ignores, of course, the mindsets reporters bring with them when they describe events or decide that an event was newsworthy in the first place.

The point in this is that in most of our international practice, and in much of our more purposeful analysis too, we make our calculations with only cursory attention to the essence of communication, that is, to the subjective meaning—and therefore *effective* meaning—that underlies overt actions and messages. By far the most important place to look if one is to understand what is going on in a communication process is the point where messages start out and end up, the place where meaning is encoded and decoded. For, as emphasized in the last chapter, meaning does not reside in what is actually seen or heard or in some inherent quality of the stimulus or symbol itself, but in what is *added* to flesh out a picture, by what "floppy disc" is in one's mental computer at the time.

Perhaps the best way to visualize how this works is to go back to the logic of the classic Rorschach, or "ink blot" test. The Rorschach test is one of the psychologist's oldest methods of finding out what goes on in our mental computers or, to use their terms, of establishing personality profiles and getting an indication of the nature of their subjects' cognitive processes. The ink blot, made by pressing drops of ink in a fold of paper, is a more or less symmetrical and randomly formed design with no meaning—which is exactly the idea. If subjects are able to describe the blots at all, they must start with the random form with its texture and color as a stimulus, *then project from the workings of their own minds any meaning that is to be found.* Whatever is seen—two witches, people talking, a butterfly, absolutely nothing—says something about what the observer is *prepared* to see. Psychologists have found by using standardized sets of these ink blots and a pretested scoring system that this device is a useful means of plumbing the personality structures of a wide range of subjects. We need not follow the technical debate regarding the Rorschach test to see that the same process of projection is what we are confronted with in working with international events and issues, which have an ink blot dimension; the observer supplies the meaning from existing mindsets. What meaning is supplied is both a function of the individual's unique cognitive processes and of the programming supplied by his culture.

This is not to urge readers to embark on their international business with handy sets of ink blots in their briefcases to "psych out" their foreign colleagues. But the procedure is highly instructive as a reminder of what is actually going on. If all parties are naturally prepared to see the same things in international "inkblots," communication about them will be improved. Even if they don't see the same things, communication can be improved simply by understanding that differences exist and, particularly, by attempting to find out what those differences are. Communication is most under control when one can predict—without thinking about it in the case of one's own culture or with conscious effort in others—what another will see in the "inkblots" of their mutual interaction. And that process, we argue, should have been possible in the case cited earlier of admitting the Shah of Iran into the U.S., which was the inkblot of that particular moment. We should have been able to predict what would be seen from the Iranian vantage point. While we might still have admitted the Shah, we would have done so with calculated precautions. More routinely, the need to predict how others will perceive something arises in discussing such things as the intent of government decisions, the fair price for an office service, the interpretation of a regulation, or the desirability of an innovation proposed in a technical assistance project.

Ink blot test aside, the essential point here is that the cognitive systems of people in the same society have, in fact, been programmed to a very considerable degree by the same agent—their culture. In that case, differences in the way issues or events are seen will be only a matter of individual variation on a theme, as people differ in their personal organization of knowledge, experiences, emotions, sense of identity, interests, moods, and all the rest. While such variation can be considerable and important, it will normally fall within acceptable limits, and therefore be understood by all concerned.

To the extent, however, that mindsets reflect the programming of differing cultures or subcultures, the possibility of significant contrasts in perception and reasoning increases enormously. Communicators must have an exceptional capacity to bridge the discrepancies.

Does this mean that we think in stereotypes and that managing stereotypes is the essence of cross-cultural communication? In popular usage, "stereotype" is a pejorative word for a dysfunctional mindset. Actually, as suggested in the last chapter, we think in stereotypes all the time to simplify the environment. So do people in other nations, and it is not necessarily bad. The question for communication purposes is the accuracy of stereotypes or the degree to which one can recognize the effect they have, be wary of them, and maintain control over them. You know you have encountered stereotyping when someone tells you that you are so nice, not at all like an American! Or vice versa.

To avoid being trapped by stereotypes, the remedy would seem to be to try to see individuals as individuals. But in doing so, we may cause the pendulum to swing too much the other way. The objective when working cross-culturally is to capture first the pattern and design of thinking that constitutes the cultural lens for people socialized in another culture. Or, better said, the objective in an international encounter is to be able first to understand the cultural lens of *each* party, oneself included, *then* focus on the individual.

Perhaps a caveat needs to be introduced at this point. In discussing the way that people are mentally programmed, the term "culture" may be used too broadly for some disciplinary tastes when the issue in question involves mindsets resulting from historical events, economic circumstances and priorities, political objectives, etc. Technically, these factors do come broadly under the definition of culture, though we feel that is a matter of choice. Perhaps we can say instead that including the perspective of the underlying cultural lens is an essential add-on to what we are already prepared to look for in explaining points of view.

In the social sciences, the inquiry into what we are calling the cultural basis for mindsets, the cultural lens, has been pursued under such designations as basic personality, modal personality, civic culture, etc. One of the best known terms is "national character," a sweeping idea in some ill-repute among social scientists for its vagueness in both the "national" and the "character" parts of the concept. It also suggests the use of psychiatric or psychoanalytic tools and ideas.

Should a practical psycho-cultural approach extend to psychiatric concepts? Ideally, the answer would be yes, for the components of the psychological process with which psychiatrists deal, i.e., basic structure and patterns of stress in personality, do come into play in understanding international behavior and are subject to cultural conditioning. Also, psychiatrists have contributed highly important insights into cross-national problems. Yet their techniques and methodologies for cross-cultural analysis and application are still in experimental stages. Their basic orientation toward working with deviant behavior and providing therapy to individuals is not necessarily transferable when applied to the interpretation of normal but foreign mindsets rather than the psychological problems of individuals out of tune with the norms of the psychiatrist's own society and culture. In any case, approaches from this field are not easily used by amateurs, either as diagnostic or conceptual tools or as a means of posing issues and problems.

International professionals have enough on their agenda in applying the more easily understandable (to laymen) ideas that come from other psycho-cultural orientations. A more reasonable approach is to use such products of psychiatric inquiry as are available for their suggestive contributions to the inquiry, but to focus first on psycho-cultural concepts that can be more readily applied to the kind of observations and information that are standard fare in the ordinary round of international activity.

This range of objectives should become clearer in the case examples below.

U.S. AND LATIN AMERICAN CULTURAL LENSES

Let us briefly demonstrate how culture supplies the programming for projecting meaning onto the world. We will do so by outlining and then comparing some of the major themes which run through U.S. and Latin American cultures. The generalizations made may need qualification or elaboration to explain variations within these broad culture areas, yet the themes mentioned are based on solid research and, taken together, illustrate distinctly contrasting ways of perceiving and reasoning between North and South Americans. We will begin with the U.S. case, which poses problems because the social structure of the United States is complex, mobile, and includes a wide variety of ethnic groups. Yet, there are basic patterns in the American outlook.

American society programs people to place an all-pervading emphasis on achievement, defining what it is, its value, and the rewards that go with it. American culture has a strong vein of optimism, at least from a cross-cultural perspective, which leads people to believe in happy endings resulting from hard work. A related belief is that problems can be solved through active effort. The U.S. is thus a management-oriented, problem-solving, activistic society. These motifs have been reflected in exploits with which Americans identify, from conquering the frontier to landing on the moon. The American life experience has led to social relations which are dominated by middle-class values and which reflect a strong egalitarian ideal and prescribe informality in personal relationships. This leads to social, physical and economic mobility that makes changing friendships and fluctuating loyalties a normal part of the experience.[6]

Growing up in the United States exposes one to the high value placed on time, efficiency, and progress; on entrepreneurship and productivity; on applied knowledge and science; and on the wealth of appliances and gadgets which science can produce. These themes have much to do with the logic of American economic life.

Political life also takes on a special quality. From childhood one hears of the public interest (a concept that does not exist everywhere), the will of the majority, the voting process. Group or social problems of all kinds are typically attacked by forming committees. One can hardly escape hearing about the process of government, from the county courthouse to the White House, or absorbing some notion of the society's feeling about the way that government functions.

The child begins to absorb these themes early on, as family experiences mold social expectations and values. Americans are usually socialized in a small nuclear family group with one to three, possibly four, children. Ten brothers and sisters or relatives other than parents in the household departs from the current norm. Even the nuclear family is threatened; growing up in a single-parent family is not at all unusual in the U.S. today.

From culturally determined child-rearing practices and similar early education experiences, American children develop shared self-concepts and perspectives. They watch the same television programs from coast to coast, are buffeted by the same advertising, and identify with American heroes, ranging from athletes to performing artists, statesmen and military leaders. They share the anxieties and the fads of their peers. They internalize from their society basic notions of ethical behavior which, while continuously changing and not always consistent, nevertheless provide in cross-cultural perspective a shared sense of right and wrong or sanctioned behavior and disapproved behavior. The conventional morality of the society is presented and reinforced in literature, churches, the editorial pages, even in the comics.

While there is disagreement about many American educational practices, the main values projected remain relatively stable. Several generations ago the most common experience included exposure to the McGuffey Reader and all the homilies that it contained. There were also Horatio Alger books and Zane Grey westerns; the romance of the frontier was still fresh. Today these authors are passé, but the optimistic pursuit of success and rugged individualism they depicted are ideals that persist, whether the context is TV dramas, space wars, science fiction, or resistance to gun control laws.

Thus, despite its extraordinary complexity and variability, there is a pattern in the way Americans are programmed to see themselves, other people, and their environment; there are common threads running through the cognitive systems of Americans as a group which form a cultural lens. These themes have to be understood by others if they would make sense out of the way Americans perceive and reason about the world. We will have occasion to refer to these themes in later chapters.

Now, for comparison, consider the Latin American cultural lens.

The Spaniards and Portuguese who came to dominate the southern portion of the Western Hemisphere brought with them their own Iberian form of society and their own Catholic notions of the way that people should relate to each other and to their physical environment. Latin America is more static when compared to North America or the dynamic nations of Europe and Asia. Emphasis is placed less on managing *things* than on managing affiliations with other people. Being who you are counts for more than what you have accomplished; security comes not from individual effort but from reciprocal relationships.

In Latin America the middle class is relatively weak, although it is developing rapidly in more industrialized urban centers. It is less likely that children will grow up in the context of what in the U.S. are called middle-class values (but which in fact are the dominant values of the American mainstream). Latin American values are determined more by elites, whose concepts of class and status are acceded to by a large peasantry or self-acknowledged working class (in some cases with strong Indian communal identities). This interrelationship tends to mold expectations regarding life style and position in the society even for the new small middle class.

Traditionally, Latin Americans tend to take a fatalistic view of events and the forces that cause them. Life and its circumstances are accepted as givens; the individual's task is to adjust to, rather than manipulate, the forces around him. Thus, class lines are not easily broken. If one is to change things, one appeals to the larger forces which are seen as life's controlling agents—the divine, the government, perhaps one's *patron*. Fate is often the central theme in Latin American literature, art, cinema, and now in the new television *novelas* which are popular. A sense of individualism is relatively strong among Latin Americans, but in contrast to North Americans, Latins define it more in terms of personal dignity rather than self-reliance, which is the dominant motif in the U.S. Friendship for Latins is rather formal, and considerable attention is given to the nurturing of substantive interpersonal relationships. Great value is placed on argumentation and debate; the idea and plan are often valued more than the practical application.

The growing child's social universe includes a large family or extended family that encompasses a broad circle of blood relatives and ceremonial family members, the *padrino* (godfather) for instance. From the beginning this social world instills in the growing child emotional ties and a perception of family relationships which result in a powerful sense of reciprocal responsibility within the family group and a commitment to family vis-a-vis the rest of the world far stronger than exists among North Americans.

Education in Latin America relates more to the enhancement of personality and social competence through the knowledge gained than to the acquisition and application of skills. The Latin ideal of leadership is based on this kind of education. The successful individual is a forceful, even audacious, personality, eloquent in expression, one who is clearly in charge and to whom other people defer, one who guards honor and who takes care of those who enter his web of personal relationships and reciprocal responsibilities. Latin Americans naturally identify with this special image of success that goes with Latin American institutional culture.

From this comparative perspective, it should be apparent that even when North and South Americans do the same thing— manage a store, teach school, direct a bureaucracy—what is done and how and why it is done will be different to the degree that they are affected by the cultural lens through which the activities are viewed and by the mindsets which come into play.

IDENTIFYING THE MINDSET FACTORS THAT ARE MOST CONSEQUENTIAL

Simply understanding that culture is the source for much of the content and design of perception and reasoning is not very helpful in actual field situations, where the number and variety of culturally molded mindsets is so large and complex—ranging from preconceptions regarding the proper way to greet a friend to the best way to generate capital investment. The next most important skill to be acquired is the ability to recognize culturally-channeled outlooks when they are facing you in ordinary behavior.

This means attending to a different level or manifestation of culture than observers are usually trained to notice. The effect of cultural lenses can be detected by noting how praise or censure is given, how children are taught, what makes people sentimental or arouses emotional reaction; it is found in humor, in cartoons, in the themes favored in literature, poetry, and especially in children's stories. The cultural lens affects the way actions are defended or rationalized, the kinds of activity that are considered strange, immoral, or a little crazy. It is to be seen in that which people take for granted, as not even cause for comment, but which seems unusual to the outsider.

Note an example of the kind of acute observation required: On being invited for dinner in a small town in the Philippines, I felt uncomfortable when the host served food but did not sit down and eat with the guests as I would expect in the spirit of fellowship and good conversation. In fact, conversation was left to the guests. The host's contribution was limited to explanations regarding the food—which for me did require explanation, to be sure. Was this unusual behavior or was it a strange custom? As the same thing happened on repeated occasions, the unusual behavior was obviously customary. But note how much more fruitful the observation is when the observer seeks out the design of the thought pattern— also customary—on which a behavior is based: a different symbolic meaning to serving food and a different sense of priorities in social interchange, a differing notion of pleasure and satisfaction, a differing definition of the occasion.

This need to discover idea patterns behind cultural behaviors applies to those who would understand Americans as well. When people from more traditional cultures observe American men helping in the kitchen, they see it through a cultural lens by which quite different role behavior is expected, and they are going to have difficulty understanding such behavior if they are unfamiliar with the American thought patterns behind it.

Sometimes customs-of-the-mind relate to the simplest of behaviors. For example, anyone who has been exposed to cross-cultural training is probably familiar with Edward Hall's insistence that cultures tune people to hold very precise ways of handling time and space.[7] I take special delight in his conclusions because I was an occasional guinea pig in Hall's pursuit of these matters when he was a senior colleague on the staff of the State Department's Foreign Service Institute. I recall his demonstrations of the way people react when their expectations of proper conversational distance are violated, when, for instance, they are talking with someone from the Middle East, where conversational distance is closer. The Americans feel so uncomfortable as they back off and try to decipher the other person's intentions that the substance of the conversation is all but lost.

Frequently, the differing meanings of even small gestures can set off a whole series of misperceptions. Minds can be programmed to expect differing formulas for expressing emotion. In business discussions Americans appear to Japanese as uncontrolled and socially incompetent when they get carried away with enthusiasm or make an argument with feeling; in turn the Japanese confuse Americans with restrained emotions and responses which do not signal inner feelings. All this contributes to a disturbing "noise level," i.e., in the terminology of communications studies, any distraction that interferes with the efficient transmission of a message.

However, most thought patterns significant to international dialogue are at least a few steps more complex. For example—another from the Philippines—consider those relating to how laws and regulations should be carried out.

Several years ago in the citizenship and passport section of the U.S. Embassy in Manila, a local resident came in requesting documentation as a U.S. citizen, claiming that one of his parents was an American. As U.S. citizenship laws had changed several times, qualifying depended on precisely when one was born. The consular officer suspected fraudulent documents, but it made little difference as the applicant did not qualify anyway, according to the date on the birth certificate presented. So he was turned down. Several days later he returned with a new birth certificate giving a different date. The combination of fraud and innocence was now obvious, but the officer restrained his righteous indignation—after all, he had been in this kind of work for some years. As it turned out, the new date also failed to qualify, which the officer pointed out. Then the applicant put the case more directly: "Please sir, you tell me when I should have been born, and I will get the certificate." A wide gulf existed in the conception of law and its purposes! And who knows on which side the angels would be found?

Many key ideas or important values carry an emotional charge. Repugnance toward what is interpreted as a violation of manners, moral principles, or religious tenets can interfere enormously with the communication process. For instance, Americans working in some traditional societies have real difficulty working with counterparts who they know are supplementing their meager official salaries with the petty graft the local system allows. When the sums are larger and the public interest is involved, it is hard to take a "cultural relativity" approach. This contrast in mindset can become a factor in international economic relations as is seen when laws governing American corporate practices abroad are debated. Paying "fees" to expedite contracts is censured in the U.S. but not necessarily elsewhere. Operating with American-based laws reflecting American preferred norms, U.S. companies often find it difficult to compete.

Reasoning itself follows differing patterns. Culture may prescribe the way that ideas are to be interconnected in patterns of logic; whether, for example, reasoning should follow an inductive and practical approach (as in the style of Galileo), a more deductive path (as Aristotle preferred) or another variation, such as French Cartesianism. These differing styles can be detected in the United Nations, where debate necessarily reflects the logic and styles of argumentation of many languages and traditions. Americans tend to become impatient with the time spent by the General Assembly discussing the exact wording of the items to be included in the agenda for each session. The American outlook suggests: "What difference does it make? We will look at the facts when we get to the actual debate." To them the title is, in effect, only a designation for deciding whether to take up the subject at all, and to serve the purposes of scheduling. The inductive approach. But to many delegations—the Russians, French and Latin Americans stand out in this regard—the act of defining the issue itself is highly important for it sets the premises by which the eventual conclusion will follow somewhat automatically in a deductive mode.

If the title says "imperialistic aggression," the line of inferences to be made and the tone of the debate follow directly; if the same matter is titled "defense of economic interests," an entirely different conclusion is to be expected. In the deductive mold, it is very important to agree on the general principles first; in the inductive, one looks at the evidence, and moves up to the principles.[8] Is one to move from the general to the particular, or the other way around? When negotiating teams address their subject from these differing preferences in logical approach, the exchange can become extraordinarily turgid. Officers who have participated in arms reduction conferences with the Soviets report that this aspect itself can delay substantive negotiations for days.

Sometimes observers too easily dismiss alien mindsets because they are "obviously" incorrect empirically. Yet, these mindsets are often deeply ingrained and affect behavior in significant ways. Whether or not they appear rational to the outsider, it is important to understand them if one is to communicate with maximum effectiveness. Some international decisionmakers, for instance, still consult astrologers before making major decisions.

Thus we see that in the course of international practice, we observe the cultural lens at work across a wide range of behavior and at different levels of abstraction. However, culturally patterned mindsets vary in the centrality of their importance in any given situation. What is needed is a way to single out those culturally-based predispositions that count most. This can best be accomplished by identifying key idea patterns which, by being fundamental to the logic of the whole cultural system, help explain other lesser assumptions and outlooks—a singling out of the limbs to which the branches necessarily attach. For example, we might suggest to foreign students that the U.S. emphasis on a competitive grading system by which students tend to be compared to each other rather than to fixed standards is logical to Americans because the larger society places high value on individual achievement, which is inevitably comparative.

To be more systematic in isolating key thought patterns, we will examine two areas where applying culturally relevant mindset analysis is especially important for international practitioners. The first is social structure; the second, institutions. Then we will consider procedures for homing in on some of the value orientations or implicit assumptions that for a given culture will make the mindsets we encounter more understandable—or, in our computer analogy, will explain the basic programming.

Social structure as a contributor to mindsets. The way a given culture defines such things as social prestige, authority, privilege, affluence, occupation and deference molds mindsets. We easily recognize international differences in class and caste. But we do not always go on to recognize that the mental programming accompanying social structures permeates the logic of international relations, economic activity and even the rationale for government and its policies. This is the source of much mismatching of mindsets in the international arena and thus merits specific emphasis here.

An all-pervading middle-class orientation tends to blind Americans to the extent to which perception can be preconditioned by a consciousness of social stratification. In world perspective, American culture in this regard is relatively unique—few societies are so middle-class in the idea patterns governing its institutions and social practices. Such emphasis as American society does place on higher or lower status is derived from credentials based largely on concrete achievements, or lack thereof, in an open and fluid social system. This contrasts with much of the rest of the world, where status is based much more on ascribed qualities.

Perhaps the most interesting situation in which outlooks on social status and roles pose difficulties is found when Americans interact with members of new middle classes in changing, formerly traditional societies. It might be expected that Americans would have difficulty relating to the old upper classes, whose view of themselves and of their prerogatives would offend American egalitarianism. They might understandably also have difficulty with the peasants, whose deference and resignation to their status would violate the American's democratic, economic and political principles. But they even have problems with the new middle sectors, skilled laborers, white-collar workers, bureaucrats, managers, professionals, school teachers, small businessmen and the like.

The difficulty lies in the fact that American outlooks stem from a middle class that has been in place and in a majority for a long time, and where "American culture" is virtually the same as "American middle-class culture." In contrast, in rapidly changing societies the new middle class enters a kind of cultural vacuum where the value base they need to support their status and position is often weak or only beginning to gel. The result is ambiguity, uncertainty and insecurity among those who occupy that position. It is harder, therefore, for overseas Americans to communicate with this group than they expect it to be. Old thought patterns and values from a more structured class system persist to confuse the American. The new middle class may, like traditional elites, look down on working with one's hands. Upper-class symbols such as titles and university degrees may receive undue emphasis. Insecurity may be reflected in the inordinate value placed on superficial aspects of modernity.

The reader will have little trouble observing class structure differences internationally. The point to be underlined here is the need to translate this phenomenon into a source of mismatched mindsets that affect international dialogue. This issue will be highlighted in later chapters, especially as we look to the psychological foundations for the *roles* that people play in institutional life and to the public mindsets out of which governments derive their logic and try to meet the expectations of their people.

Mindsets and institutions.   Mindsets relating to institutions are of strategic importance to practitioners because so much of the day-to-day work internationally involves institutions, be they governmental, political, social or economic. Later chapters will focus more specifically on some of these institutions, but there is a central point to be made here that ties the cultural lens idea to institutional analysis. Its essence is that the way institutions are *interrelated within a cultural system* affects the way that people are programmed to think about any specific institution, be it marriage or the civil service. The full rationale of comparative sociological analysis cannot be condensed into a short summary, but the key idea is that mindsets which determine how institutions will be perceived and reasoned about by a native of the system will reflect that person's experience with the way that the institution in question fits into the culture's larger, functionally interconnected system of institutions.

We know that an institution like the civil service is not understood in the same way in the United States, Great Britain, and India, although these civil services are formally and technically similar. People who deal with them sense special nuances and expect differing bureaucratic practices and even different spoken and unspoken objectives. In part this is because these national civil services do operate differently. But it is also due in part to an absorbed sense of the larger system which is superimposed, usually unconsciously, on one's expectations. As one thinks "civil service," somewhere on the edge of one's consciousness is an awareness of particular interconnected legal practices, religious institutions and the values that go with them, political institutions and their practices, and much more to flesh out perceptions. What one does is superimpose a sense of institutional *context* onto an understanding of civil service—and this will not be the same in the three societies cited.

In this example, British government itself has always been a more central part of the institutional system, more "royal" and imperial and encompassing in its authority. Elite educational institutions dedicate themselves to producing competent civil servants. Family prestige comes with having a hand in governing. Thus, inside the system one senses a consistency and a feeling of propriety and self-assurance in carrying out its functions that is less pronounced in the American system. The American civil service is seen by its citizens as a more tolerated than honored necessity, as the government itself is granted a more limited mission. It is less elitist and more egalitarian in outlook as it reflects the world's foremost middle-class social structure. In the climate of the American working culture, it is a little more individualistic and its members are better paid, as the business world competes for its personnel. Also reflecting the larger American cultural system, the civil service is more likely to judge itself and be judged by standards of efficiency and practical application, and perhaps less by its sense of loyalty and ethical steadfastness.

In the case of India, simply pointing out that the society is one which educates more professionals than the job market can accommodate and has no effective state-supported social security system suggests a special view of the civil service. It offers career security in a social structure in which other kinds of security are hard to find. In this circumstance, a large civil service that attends to detail beyond the demands of efficiency might be a virtue; more are accommodated, i.e., are provided security.

Simply comparing institutions cross-nationally, isolated from the context of their systems, is rather naive, like trying to compare pieces from different jigsaw puzzles without taking into account all the other pieces from the respective puzzles that give meaning to the individual piece.

In effect, we are looking for ways to anticipate patterns of subjective meaning an institution will have for the people who deal with it in its specific cultural environment. When people relate to an institution or its practices, they do so with a supporting composite of pertinent images that go well below the surface facts. If the subjective meaning of single words or phrases can differ, it is obvious that the fully rounded-out meaning or mental picture of still more abstract institutions will vary with contrasting cultural and national experience.

In the final analysis, the nature of the cultural lens will be affected not only by the formal and obvious purposes and functions of institutions, but also by a sense of *latent* function unique to the system in question. That is, the lens will embody the more subtle ways the institution in question is affected by the system and, in turn, the subtle effects it has on other parts of the system.

As an example of the latent function, consider churches as institutions within a system. There are Episcopal churches in both the American South and in South Africa. The obvious or manifest function of churches in both systems is to provide for and sustain religious practices; yet, in these two social systems, other functions that religious institutions have will be important in understanding the meaning of being Episcopalian in each culture, which is not the same. In the American South being an Episcopalian tends to reflect high social standing in the white community. In South Africa, membership is largely in the black community; understanding the Episcopal church there requires also understanding such political institutions as apartheid, to which the church must relate. Or to carry the religious institution example further, in the Middle East, Islamic practices have a *latent* function in the way that banks operate. Lending money and collecting interest conflict with religious doctrine. So, interest is called something else and handled in special ways—which from outside the system is more or less unintelligible, but which is natural and customary for those inside the system.

So, studying banks and churches becomes something like studying physiology; we may be interested in the anatomy of the lungs, but lungs make a lot more sense when studied in functional interrelationship with with the rest of the organs of the body—the system.

Skill in sorting out how mindsets take institutional *systems* into account is a distinct advantage. Competent homework in the form of area studies is especially important in this connection. The task is to apply what we already know as "systems analysis," but at the level of psychological process.

Value orientations as basic programming. "Value orientations" is the term often used to designate basic assumptions, often emotionally laden, which by their saliency give integration to a cultural system. Taken together, values comprise much of the cultural lens and form the basis and establish the "givens" for mindsets. "Values" is not an altogether satisfactory term; many core assumptions are not necessarily values in the sense of being positive goals or ethical prescriptions for the society. However, the term does point toward a focus on the thought patterns that, in accord with the computer analogy, are the most important in setting our basic mental programming. Put differently, in a way that better captures the essence of the "cultural lens," we are looking for the deeply rooted thought patterns in a given culture that go the furthest to shape the cultural lens.

The main point here is that there are central themes, philosophical threads, and enduring assumptions that run through a culture to give it consistency and design, and a logic for behavior.

Let us illustrate by noting several case examples involving values, starting with achievement motivation in the United States. It would be difficult for a foreign visitor to understand American behavior in any depth without attention to the value placed on achievement. Admittedly, as seen from the inside, this value is changing. Achievement is declining in some sectors as a driving force in American life, or it is becoming inconsistent with certain aspects of current social reality. The thesis of Max Weber's classic *The Protestant Ethic and the Spirit of Capitalism* may require some qualification.

But from the outside looking in, achievement motivation serves as a convenient entry point in examining American "national character" and in attempting to understand the logic of personal behavior, the nature of community activity, the dynamics of the economic system, the meaning of success, the granting of social prestige, the forms of democratic practice and the way that money and material possessions serve as potent symbols of achievement. Understanding the way that achievement is defined leads one to appreciate the role of competition in American society and the value placed on work and on applied knowledge.

The significance of the achievement motive was brought to the fore some years ago by social psychologist David McClelland and his colleagues in studies comparing achievement motivation in various societies. He suggested that the core value serving as a stimulus to entrepreneurship and economic development in the U.S. was the need to achieve. It constituted a kind of psychological mainspring, culturally transmitted and not necessarily found in the same form in other societies.[9] Its absence or de-emphasis in the cultures of less developed countries, he argued, might be an inhibiting factor in their attaining desired levels of economic development, at least if entrepreneurship were to be the formula.

This consideration does not ordinarily appear in economic models of development.

This theme will be pursued further in Chapter Six. It is mentioned here to illustrate our conceptual train of thought. Achievement motivation is a very consequential value; it affects the nature of the entire socio-cultural system. A change in this one value would have the effect of altering a whole complex of key assumptions by which other interconnected parts of the culture function. It would change the basic programming.

Differing values lead to differing definitions of "success." Again, compare U.S. culture with that of Latin America. In his *The Public Man—An Interpretation of Latin American and Other Catholic Countries*,[10] Glen Dealy argues that the whole complex of values by which people pattern their aspirations will differ between Protestant-oriented cultures, such as the United States, and Catholic-oriented societies, such as those found in Latin America, Italy and Spain. Thus, on the one hand, in the U.S. personal success is reached through achievement, which emphasizes a drive to get things done, accumulate capital, and produce goods and services in order to gain status and wealth. In Latin America the satisfactions sought are more tuned to the acquisition of a kind of social power. Success consists of *being* someone personally important, of being surrounded by other people who are dependent in some way, who recognize the importance of and extend deference to this form of social accomplishment.

Work *per se* holds little value; indeed, it is to be avoided. Developing friendships and connections, on the other hand, is a form of capital investment in one's career; the degree to which one appears powerful and important consitutes one's credit rating in the society. An assured and genteel use of leisure gives status, rather like projecting an image of being busy and efficient would in the U.S. Style is everything; manliness counts and is to be displayed; dignity and honor assume a special meaning and importance.

Dealy's thesis is that the Latin American behavior which outsiders often see as irrational is, in fact, very rational and predictable if the central value orientations of the culture are appreciated, if customary behavior is understood in terms of the central "public man" logic of the society. He notes that while the wealthy and welleducated have the advantage in these countries, the desire to "be someone" rather than simply "do something" extends to the village and the family as well. Across the culture it is as much a psychological mainspring for their brand of success as achievement motivation is for North Americans.

Other samples of central values that supply the logic for a way of life come readily to mind. In the Philippines there is an especially heightened and pervading concern with reciprocity; a particularly high value is placed on properly honoring obligations. This parallels the Latin American case to a large extent. The good life is seen as living in a secure human network in which one is bound to and protected by obligations. Thus, a local villager feels morally quite comfortable in voting for the politician whose influence has directed public works funds to that village or perhaps has even provided jobs for relatives, as a result of which the villager has accepted a customary reciprocal responsibility. This is not a deviation from political ethics, it *is* the ethic. Many other important Philippine cultural patterns involve techniques for remembering details of the reciprocity net and for fulfilling reciprocal demands. Hence, while this political practice may seem to be paralleled in other societies, it has a special sanction in Philippine culture.

In Japan, a similar but much more elaborate conception of honoring obligation and debt explains much of the logic of Japanese behavior, even to a corporation manager's personal acceptance of blame for company errors, or the proper resort to suicide, a theme of traditional Japanese literature and films. Family relations, labor and management affairs, and respect for the emperor all ride on intricate and conventional ways of assuming and discharging personal and group obligation. Not surprisingly, the Japanese language is endowed with numerous honorifics which imply degrees and kinds of mutual obligation. This makes the language especially difficult for Westerners, for not only must they learn the basic honorifics, but also the cultural programming behind them that establishes the social meaning.

It can be argued that much of the difference in approach to social, economic and political affairs between the United States and the Soviet Union derives from opposite value emphases. Does the programming for mindsets start with primary concern for the individual or for the group? The American approach places value first on the individual, which sets the philosophical pattern for American religion, law, social structure, government, education, etc. Russian culture, on the other hand, values the well-being of the group, from which the well-being of the individual is derived. Thus emerges a contrasting logic for the functioning of law, government, and economic institutions. It leads a Russian to internalize a quite different sense of individuality, different aspirations and expectations regarding social relations and the role of authority. We will refer to this issue again in a later chapter.

Another way of identifying the relatively more significant and consequential elements that serve as foundation blocks for culture's basic programming is to call them "deep culture." Thus, from the examples above, achievement motivation, reciprocity, and group orientation are part of the deep culture of Americans, Filipinos, and Russians respectively. Like the roots of a plant, they are to be found below the surface but they sustain surface culture and give it the special qualities that one can see, describe, and talk about. Deep culture is internalized and does not ordinarily need to be examined or questioned; it is the foundation for basic beliefs, for common sense and conventional wisdom. Typically, it is well established before the age of five or six. Edward Stewart, of the International Christian University in Tokyo, who called my attention to this way of expressing the culture's basic programming, finds that many of the sharp contrasts in Japanese and American management styles and production processes are explainable when attention is directed to contrasts in deep culture.

A caution regarding using generalizations of this kind might be useful here. It would be a mistake to reject or downplay the significance and effect of deeply rooted cultural assumptions and values simply because it is so often apparent that *not all* Germans, Italians, or Chinese are alike. One should not allow the ample evidence of individual variation to obscure the fundamentals. If, for example, something like the degree of felt need to achieve or to value reciprocity networks were placed on a scale and a statistical curve were drawn to show where most members of a society would score, the high modes of the curves would clearly differ from culture to culture. Thus, it is productive to know first how the curves and modes vary by culture, as this establishes what one is most likely to encounter. Individual variation can then be taken into account as a second step.

It might be assumed that in much modern international work, difficulties caused by differing value orientations will be greatly diminished because international professionals are, after all, cosmopolitan people, quite experienced in communicating with each other. In addition they are fortified by conventional ways of handling international problems that have been around for a long time. Supposedly, members of international communities share mutual assumptions regarding issues and a certain rationality, both of which reduce the cross-cultural distance between them to a matter of little consequence. But it is not usually that easy; several factors tend to guarantee that culturally related mindsets will still be at work.

In the first place, the professional men and women who participate in international decision making and negotiation are still quite susceptible to cultural influence. Despite their socialization in the rarified atmosphere of international diplomacy or multinational corporations and the objectivity which is expected of them in their jobs, they inevitably share to some degree the mindsets of their particular societies and identify with the interests and outlooks of the publics they represent. Their views of issues and events can never be totally divorced from this fact. Few completely impartial brokers exist in the international negotiation arena, and they probably would not be trusted to represent their national clients in any case.

We might note parenthetically that there may now be exceptions in multinational corporations where certain supranational outlooks may have become the conventional wisdom of international managers. It is also to be recognized that international affairs enjoys the presence of an ever increasing number of bicultural personalities—people whose cross-cultural experience allows them to switch, in effect, from one deep culture to another. To the extent that they can manage the shift psychologically, they become the true internationalists and thus invaluable as go-betweens in bridging cultures.

Secondly, with increasing public participation in the broad range of foreign affairs activities, decision makers are relatively limited to making those decisions which make some sense to their involved public. Decisions must respond to popular perceptions of the issues and to popular objectives. Both decisions and tactics have to fall within the public's tolerable limits of morality or national self-image. These limits differ markedly, of course, from one society to another, and the tactics and objectives of the world's leaders vary accordingly, even though they may personally prefer to adhere to the established conventions of international negotiation and problem-solving.

Finally, as few policies in any country are the creations of single individuals, the opinions and beliefs of the group will enter into the making of decisions and the choosing of tactics by the mere fact that it is a group process. At the least, a staff discusses and interprets pertinent information, thus multiplying the number of personalities involved and reflecting the mindsets of the larger society in reaching a decision. At the upper end of the scale of group involvement within the governmental process, congresses and parliaments are also culturally programmed and may engage in extended debate on an issue before a decision is made or an agreement ratified. This can happen in private institutions as well, among stockholders, executives, members, or other constituencies.

When it comes to policy execution, group mindsets continue to affect behavior, for whether it is an army, an embassy, or a field staff that is charged with policy execution, the policy is still carried out by groups of culturally-bound people. They reinforce each other in the "common sense" of their society as they determine the style with which the policy is to be executed and the adaptations and adjustments that have to be made in actual application. In turn, those in the field report back on the policy's fortunes and give their view of situations requiring further decisions. Again, their interpretations will be affected by the subjective subtleties of group dynamics, and the purity of the decision-making process yields further to a group-reinforced cultural influence. For better or for worse, the influence of group wisdom is particularly apparent in democratic societies and in governments where the committee and the inter-agency group approach is most relied upon in judging issues and making decisions. Here the connection between national behavior and "deep culture" is most likely to be reinforced.

CHAPTER FOUR

The Fine Art of Diagnosing Mindsets—A Checklist

INTRODUCTION

Now that our basic theoretical propositions have been presented, we will turn to their application. The test of what has been set forth so far is whether it can be used to diagnose contrasting perceptions in the context of both fast-moving international situations and routine international activities.

For the purpose of helping the international practitioner, we offer a checklist of questions to guide the reader in applying psycho-cultural concepts to the analysis of real international events and cross-cultural interactions to search out the effect differing mindsets may be having on them. While this checklist is not intended to be a substitute for scientific research, it should be a useful tool in enabling practitioners, especially as participant observers, to systematically ask the right questions.

Diagnosing mindsets cross-culturally is not an easy exercise. There is no bird watcher's handbook available that lists and describes all the varieties one is likely to encounter. But having at one's disposal a set of questions that will lead to accurate diagnoses (or at least informed guesses), no matter what specific cultures or mindsets are involved, should be helpful. The checklist approach is simply a means of expanding one's powers of observation and interpretation.

In arriving at the lead questions forming the framework for this chapter, both mindset theory and typical field difficulties involving psycho-cultural complications have been taken into consideration. Heaviest emphasis will be placed on perception factors that derive from cultural differences, since that will be the newest ground for most readers. It is well to remember, however, that there are many sources for contrasting patterns of thinking and behaving—historical and economic factors, for example—that are more easily apparent and less complex than the deeply rooted cultural patterns implanted in people by the process of acculturation. The "fine art" of diagnosing mindsets, therefore, consists at least in part in being able to distinguish the factors that influence mindsets and the operational levels at which these influences work. We will start out listing questions in outline form before offering more detailed commentary. Our list will move from the more to the less obvious, starting with the least culturally mysterious factors which pertain to situation and context. Then we move on to questions regarding the way that differences in information bases lead to differing perceptions. Considered next are the effects of images, then cultural and social determinants. Finally, we will look at the more particular influences of individual personality and group dynamics.

THE CHECKLIST

Situation and context

1. How do obvious differences in *historical, geographical or economic facts of life* translate into a special pattern of priorities and concerns?

2. How does the *context* in which issues are presented affect the way they are perceived or their dramatic or emotional impact?

3. Do any *unanticipated higher priority concerns or hidden agendas* influence perception of the issue at hand?

Knowledge and information base

4. What *knowledge or information* base do people bring to the issue or event?

5. What is the effect of *new information*, such as that coming from the media or other channels?

6. What *myths* (including historical ones) are included in the information base on each side?

The image factor

7. What *images of the other side* require consideration?

8. What *national self-images* help explain reactions to issues or events?

9. Are *images of the international system* and of its operations at significant variance?

Cultural and social determinants: the cultural lens

10. Are there mismatches in *deep cultural beliefs, values, or assumptions?*

11. Does anything about the issue or event elicit *strong emotional reactions because of the cultural lens* through which it is viewed?

12. Does experience with differing *social structures* and the *related role behaviors* that go with them affect perception of the issue?

13. What effect does experience with differing *institutional forms, functions and operations* have?

14. To what extent are differing *styles of logic and reasoning* apparent? Are they reflected in language?

Individual personality and group dynamics

15. To what extent does the *uniqueness of individual personality and experience* need to be taken into account?

16. Are any special *styles of group dynamics, information processing, or decision making* present?

Notations on a checklist approach

As mentioned above, we recognize the difference between using a checklist and conducting more sophisticated research. In the case of fast-breaking international events, too often the issue has already been addressed by the time the research, with its more elaborate methodology, is completed and the results made available. The point of decision making is overtaken by events. A checklist, however, has immediate applicability. It is the procedure used by the pilot of an airplane to check all the systems of the airplane prior to takeoff. Thus, possible problems can be identified and corrected while something can be done about them. Similarly, the checklist offered here should help the international practitioner identify and either avoid or at least prepare for potential trouble spots or conflicts in international negotiations or interaction before they occur.

A few general points apply to the use of the checklist. First, it is essential to identify just whose mindsets are being diagnosed: those of a government, one of its officials, a political party, a company, the public? Or perhaps your own? Whatever the choice for the purpose at hand, and whether it be that of an individual, a group, or a whole nation, the key strategy suggested here is to consider the perceivers first as adherents of underlying perception patterns that characterize the base culture or subculture, and *then* consider within that perspective idiosyncratic factors such as qualities of individual personality or aspects of group dynamics unique to the specific situation. As discussed earlier, this is a reversal of usual procedure, but when one is working internationally, it is essential. In many situations it may be difficult to decide which of several sets of perceivers to focus on first. The rule of thumb is to start with the central figures or groups involved and work out from there.

Second, one has to be precise in defining the central subject (issue or event) that elicits differing patterns of perception and reasoning, and then branch out to such other issues as are germane. Issues or events rarely occur in isolation; there will be several balls in the air at once. But orderly procedure demands clarity at the outset in knowing what subject, or part of a subject, calls for the diagnosis.

Third, if the purpose is an objective understanding of the nature of the gap between points of view, a *two-way comparative* approach is required. This means giving equal emphasis to exploring mindsets on each side. As a participant observer, one must remember that one's own point of view may constitute half or more of the reason for any breakdown that occurs.

Fourth, in any given situation, the questions posed here will probably not be of equal importance or lead to equally significant insights. Different and potentially more useful questions will probably come to mind, depending on the problem. The less germane of our questions can be put aside, but they will have served their purpose as a first step in narrowing the field.

We will now discuss each checklist question separately. In the chapters which follow, the questions will be seen as threads weaving through the issues under discussion.

Situation and context

1. *How do obvious differences in historical, geographical or economic facts of life translate into a special pattern of priorities and concerns?* This question is the logical starting point. Most simply, it is country background study—history, climate, geography, economy and resources, international connections, etc.—translated into psychological consequences. This is where an ability to empathize goes a long way.

It is obvious that the perspective on the East-West arms race will be different for those living in Central Europe with little power to intervene, or for those in the Third World where economic development is the all-important issue than it will for those living in either of the super powers. The mind focuses differently on Middle Eastern politics according to whether or not one is dependent on Middle Eastern oil. Having experienced a war fought inside one's own city produces an outlook quite unlike that held in places where soldiers left to fight somewhere else. Living in a country where the economy is largely dependent on a single export product like bananas, coffee, tin, or sugar produces a different pattern of concerns and anxieties than living in a multi-faceted economy not dependent on any one item.

I recall a diplomat returning from a tour in Egypt. During his time there he sensed a mood of reluctant resignation in accepting international technical and economic assistance and wondered what it must feel like to be a citizen of a country renowned as the cradle of civilization, where tourists come from around the world to marvel at its relics, and yet which is now beholden to outsiders for the competence needed to manage in the modern world? This is a good example of the approach we are recommending in this book: the observer knew the basic circumstances, used his experience thoughtfully, added empathy, and translated it all into a sense of an Egyptian mindset.

The point is that in diagnosing mindsets, there is a need to translate the factual information readily available into the living, breathing assumptions and front-of -the-mind concerns that people carry with them into international encounters. Or, put the other way around, because of the tendency to project, it is easy to overlook the degree to which our own perspectives are based on our unique national experience, leaving us vulnerable to the assumption that our concerns must be everybody's concerns.

Note that this question poses a mindset problem even when cultural considerations are relatively less germane, especially when the issue involves such matters as exchange rates and balance of payments, export and import regulations, defense planning, standards of living, or technology transfers.

2. *How does the context in which issues are presented affect the way they are perceived or their dramatic or emotional impact?* This is a question from basic perception psychology. How an item is perceived is in part a function of the larger context in which it is presented. Therefore, the practical goal is to try to anticipate the perceiver's probable sense of context. As noted in one of our examples above, a military exercise may be seen as a routine maneuver or a threatening gesture, depending on what else is going on at the same time. A foreign trade restriction will be seen as far more unfair when one's own factories are being closed down than when some other nation's economy is being threatened.

As discussed earlier, context can be so compelling that a "reality" may be perceived that does not even exist, especially if that context is dramatic or evokes strong emotion. Consider, for example, the World War II episode in which Americans of Japanese descent were herded into internment camps as a security precaution. In the context of the Japanese attack on Pearl Harbor, the sense of an overpowering threat was projected onto anything that looked Japanese. In the process, Japanese American motives and loyalties were grossly misperceived.

Hence, in diagnosing reactions to issues and events, such considerations as (1) who it is that raises an issue, (2) the context within which it is reported, (3) what other issues it becomes associated with, and 4) what people are generally concerned about at the time, all become significant questions to pursue.

3. *Do any unanticipated higher priority concerns or hidden agendas influence perception of the issue at hand?* In looking for explanations for positions taken by a counterpart, wise negotiators take into account concerns or priorities that on the surface may have nothing to do with the subject under discussion. The point advocated

may not tell the whole story; somewhere there may be more encompassing objectives or constraints which bear on the negotiation. There may be an agenda hidden from the observer either intentionally or otherwise.

Consider the problem that an official in a developing country might have in understanding the hidden, or at least hard to explain, agenda in the back of the minds of U.S. Agency for International Development officials in discussing, let us say, a new, relatively small loan project for constructing agricultural schools. Among all the concerns about making school projects successful, the USAID representatives know that they will have to comply with as many as one hundred distinct U.S. statutory requirements before such a loan project can be processed through their own bureaucratic mill. They know that these requirements will range from environmental impact studies to balance of payment technicalities, to certification that equipment will be shipped on a U.S. flag carrier, to a check-off with political policies. They thus have an understandable aversion to small projects—the bureaucratic work load may be out of proportion to the merit of the activity being considered. Local counterpart officials would have a difficult time anticipating all these angles carried in the minds of the American team in what otherwise would seem to be a straightforward proposition!

The task for one anticipating mindset complications is to identify these interconnected concerns or hidden agendas. Does one's counterpart have a political debt to pay, a budget to stay within? Do bureaucrats compete with other parts of their bureaucracy for influence? Are there critics in the background that have to be placated?

Again, this is a case in which exercising empathy and doing one's homework in understanding the larger context for decision making pay off. It can hardly be overdone. However, cynics charge that some traditional diplomats get carried away in their search for the hidden and devious element; they become so preoccupied with concealed objectives that they can never take a straightforward position as valid! The classic example is the diplomat who is supposed to have asked darkly when a member of an opposing negotiating team suddenly died of a heart attack, "Now what was behind that?"

Knowledge and information base

4. *What knowledge or information base do people bring to the issue or event?* In calculating the way someone is programmed to pursue a subject under discussion, an obvious approach is to ask what information base that person is working from. This includes both the information currently being obtained from news reports, briefings, the media, discussions with colleagues etc., and the longer-standing accumulation of information or baseline knowledge from which you or your counterpart must draw for understanding and interpreting the issue at hand. Some pertinent questions include: Is the perceiver equipped with extensive or limited knowledge of the subject? Is that knowledge accurate? How much comes from educational background? How much from experience, and what kind of experience? What is the cumulative result of all this input?

The point is that how well two people communicate depends in part on the compatibility of their relevant knowledge bases. In the case of international dialogue between specialists and technical experts there is often a relatively large shared domain of well-synchronized knowledge. But in less structured encounters, background knowledge may not be so well matched. Ignoring the question or making the conscious assumption that there is a shared knowledge base leaves one vulnerable to mismatched mindsets functioning on radically different and/or culturally determined information bases.

5. *What is the effect of new information, such as that coming from the media or other channels?* Most international relations are conducted in an environment saturated with new information coming from any number of channels, though normal news flow is the most immediate and obvious one. In fact issues themselves often are, if not actual creations of the media, at least significantly dependent on media treatment. A number of the terrorist acts committed in recent years constitute salient examples.

For our purposes there are two lines of analysis to pursue. The first is relatively simple: how does new information itself add to or affect the base knowledge and conditioning from which one perceives and reasons about issues? Here the question becomes *what* new information has reached the perceiver, where has it come from, and how does that information predispose one to look at the problem at hand. For example, even those decision makers who have access to the most sophisticated information sources, such as government intelligence agencies or business analytical services, will still get new information from the press or media with all the potential inherent in these sources for the influencing of meaning.

To see how this works internationally, compare the accounts of a given event as carried in the press of two different countries. If one examines the content of British and Argentine papers during the 1982 Falkland/Malvinas crisis, or of Cuban and American papers during the aborted Bay of Pigs invasion in 1963, it is difficult to believe the same event was being covered in each of the newspapers. In sum, while few people operate internationally only on the basis of "all I know is what I read in the papers," the course and content of new information, including propaganda, is a highly important element in international communication.

The second line of analysis is much more complex because it involves the very mindsets one is trying to understand in the first place. That is, the *end effect* of new information, whatever its source or content, is subject to the way the information is processed by the cognitive systems of the people involved. This brings us full circle: while new information adds to the knowledge base of the cognitive system and affects the perceptual process, *how* it adds to that cognitive system depends on the workings of the programmed mindset taking it all in. As noted in Chapter II, what is perceived in new information and the meaning assigned to it are functions of the way the cognitive system decodes the message. To penetrate this complex circle of learning and perceiving, it may help to use the evidence of people's responses to new information as a clue to the nature of the mindset at work. Does the person or group in question believe the new information? What part of it seems to attract the most attention? How is the new information interpreted? By taking this evidence into consideration, one can, in effect, work backwards to get some picture of the pattern of beliefs, values, concerns, etc., that have affected information processing, that is, to recreate the mindset that has been applied.

6. *What myths (including historical ones) are included in the information base on each side?* We have stressed that people respond to reality not necessarily as it is, but according to their image of that reality. Therefore, myths may be fully operative mindset factors.

One needs not only to take them into account, but to resist downplaying their importance just because they may be empirically untrue.

It can be argued, for example, that in 1973, after Egyptian forces had crossed the Suez Canal to attack Israeli forces, they were finally saved from disaster only by outside intervention. Their overall success was not particularly striking as seen from the outside. But the way the event was perceived and remembered inside Egypt was quite the opposite. The canal was successfully crossed and the Egyptian armed forces did perform competently by modern military standards. This became the boost in self-esteem that was necessary for the subsequent Sadat mission to Israel and for supporting the peace treaty that followed. That the new Egyptian perceptions of themselves and of their enemy were based on a degree of myth or subjective interpretation of the event does not detract from the importance of those perceptions in making accommodation with Israel thinkable—where it had not been before.

Certainly the reciprocal Soviet and American "knowledge" of each other contains a mixture of myth and subjectively remembered history which, distorted or not, plays an important part in the nuclear standoff. Public myths were the cause of considerable tension, when the late Governor Rockefeller—whose name abroad means Standard Oil—came to visit Bolivia during my time there. While the truth was that (a) the Gulf Oil Company (then in deep public relations troubles with the Bolivian government and people) was *not* a subsidiary of Standard Oil, and (b) the Chaco War, in which Bolivia's losses to the Paraguayans were heavy, had not been bankrolled by Standard Oil, myths to the contrary were part of the public information base. As a result, angry protesters attacked several U.S. Consulate installations in provincial Cochabamba, much to our discomfort.

The diagnostic objective is to take both one's own and other people's myths seriously. It is too easily assumed that merely citing the facts by chapter and verse will dispel the other's myths. But the psychological process does not work that way. Note American resistance to abandoning the myths surrounding the Chiang Kai-Shek government in China, even when contradicted by the evidence. The so-called China Lobby, with public support, carried a distorted view into policy for years. Or consider the American attitude toward their occupation of the Philippines at the end of the last century which was (and still is) seen essentially as benevolent and self-sacrificing, as part of a manifest destiny to bring enlightenment and democracy to that part of the world. Neither the hard facts of history not the negative Philippine attitude—which also includes myths—toward the occupation has changed the American mindset in any large degree. A book with the title *Little Brown Brothers* (irony intended) which tried to put our rule over the Philippines into more objective perspective made relatively little impact[1]. It was not what Americans wanted to hear. Ironically, this ethnocentric outlook was probably a significant factor in the outrage Americans felt over the cumulative excesses of the Marcos government, resulting in their support for his removal in 1986.

The image factor

7. *What images of the other side require consideration?* This issue is already generally recognized as an important subject, one that deserves more careful attention than it usually receives. Literature on the role of images in international relations is extensive. Subjects researched and analyzed range from the images one country holds of another, particularly an enemy, to promoting favorable images of one's own country. This latter aim has been a fundamental consideration in establishing such programs as the Peace Corps, the Fulbright Program and cultural exchanges. Images often constitute key elements in the way international events unfold, as in Iranian images of the United States (The Great Satan) during the hostage crisis or Japanese images of the U.S. before Pearl Harbor.

For the person working internationally, it is helpful to look to the *source* of images as a way of understanding what they are and what impact they have. Thus, one might follow with a more critical eye the content of imported television programs, the presence of one's compatriots in a given country as tourists, troops stationed abroad, missionaries, or students. The image-producing content of newspaper coverage, of literature, or intentional propaganda becomes important in such a review.

If, for example, an observer were trying to discern the American image of Asian countries, it would be useful to know that in an analysis of textbooks used by American school children, the Asia Society found that Asian countries were presented in a Western-oriented, ethnocentric frame of reference. Disproportionate stress was placed on Asian "backwardness" and on the lack of progress in modernization and the incompetence implied by that condition[2].

8. *What national self-images help explain reactions to issues or events?* Images of self are just as important as images of others. National identity and pride, a sense of place in history, popular beliefs about the role of the nation in the contemporary world—all have a major effect on mindsets, indeed are mindsets in themselves. They establish who people think they are, individually and collectively, and go a long way in explaining national policies, reactions to international events, and, ultimately, the definition of national interests which influence national behavior.

One place where self-images stand out in abundance and in close juxtaposition is in the United Nations and its committees and agencies. The nature of the national self-image of almost any country could be deduced from the way its delegations go about their business in the UN. Member delegations choose their style of participation, push items for the agenda, and align themselves in blocs significantly in accord with national self-images. Such images also affect the substance of debate and tactics used for persuasion.

Colonialism has left its stamp on self-images that cannot be avoided in diagnosing international affairs. In many former colonies the sense of being violated, denegrated, disadvantaged, and unfairly dependent has become part of a complex psychological predisposition that has assumed an almost overriding importance in the way that international issues are viewed. On the other hand, while one-time colonial empires have lost their former status, their self-image as benevolent mentors persists. The French, for instance, place great stock in perpetuating French Culture in their former spheres of influence. The British emphasize proper British procedure and style when they transfer authority to new administrations in their former colonies.

National self-images are not terribly difficult to identify. As one clue, they are hinted at in heroic legends, myths, stories and songs. By way of illustration, could the American self-image be understood without capturing the feeling that goes with the legends of western expansion? The British without knighthood? The Australian without the Outback? The Spanish without El Cid?

9. *Are images of the international system and of its operations at significant variance?* Images held of the international system itself, or on some aspect of its operation, color outlooks on specific issues and events. Therefore, mindsets that relate to them need to be explored.

Note, for example, the polarization that occurred when debate began on Third World demands for a new international economic order. The view of the system was a fundamental element. The mindsets of people preoccupied with colonial dependence contrasted sharply with those of people seated in the offices of major international business and economic institutions. Similarly, the image of the international security system and the way it operates differs significantly between the superpowers and the countries caught in between.

Remember once again to consider both the source and content of images, and remember also that the accuracy of the image is beside the point; myth or misperception can be as powerful in forming outlooks as facts and figures.

Cultural and social determinants: the cultural lens

10. *Are there mismatches in deep cultural beliefs, values, or assumptions?* This question refers to the basic ideas that were discussed in the last chapter. It asks what aspects of life are taken for granted and what implicit assumptions support feelings regarding the way things *ought* to be, what is right and wrong, normal and abnormal, true and false.

This is one of the more demanding questions on the checklist, for it addresses deep culture—the fundamentals of religion, formal and informal philosophy, and ideology as internalized in the thought patterns of those reacting to international matters. Such behavior cannot be readily observed; it has to be deduced from the spoken word or overt actions.

It would be helpful if anthropologists could supply some agreed-upon layman's guide to itemizing, probing and comparing the contents of deep culture, but such over-simplification could be as misleading as helpful. There is, however, a means of establishing a rationale for the search and thus of organizing one's field observations. That is to start with the fundamental aspects of human existence which cry out for culture's master programming and , with this lead, look for the underlying patterns of thinking and reasoning that form the deep culture of a given society. For example, how "time" is to be conceptualized and used is a universal question. Culture comes to the rescue, leading those conditioned to its particular ways to think of time as, perhaps, linear, or cyclical, or to emphasize the past, the present, or the future, or some combination of the above.

A number of these aspects of cultural programming are frequently singled out for cross-cultural comparison and can be useful guides for the international practitioner. Some samples:

- How is the relationship between the individual and the physical world conceptualized?
- Can the individual control his environment or should he be submissive to the course of events on the assumption that larger forces will prevail?
- Can one plan for and affect the future?
- Is work basically good, bad, or simply to be suffered?
- How do individuals perceive their relationships with other people?
- What is a "family"—who is included , how is it organized, and what sentiments are involved?
- How does one relate to authority, to society's moral codes, to law?
- How does the culture program one to think about those events and forces that defy explanation from direct experience and thereby cause anxiety because of their unpredictability or devastating effect—disease, death, changes of season, typhoons. Is science the guide? Religious prescriptions? Some of Both?

Many current international problems call attention to the role of deep culture. Introducing birth control, negotiating human rights, estimating the moral basis of leadership in another country, urging private entrepreneurship versus a more collective economic approach are examples.

This search for components of deep culture and their significance in foreign affairs will be demonstrated in more detail in the following chapters. It is worth mentioning here that taking deep culture into account has produced some successes in the past. At the end of World War II, for example,the question of what should be done with the Emperor of Japan arose. Should he be treated as a war criminal or as a symbol of national identity and cohesion, which was needed for rehabilitation of the defeated country. The decision required a careful sorting out of the deep and differing value orientations of the winners and losers. He was, of course, retained as emperor, and few would doubt today that it was a fortuitous decision, even though many changes were imposed on the Emperorship as an institution. Four decades later, at the 1986 Economic Summit Conference in Tokyo, his presence was still a symbol of Japan's dignity and hospitality as he joined in proceedings that included heads of state from Europe and America.

11. *Does anything about the issue or event elicit strong emotional reaction because of the cultural lens through which it is viewed?* The course of an international exchange often involves subjects which evoke deep, emotionally charged, culturally programmed convictions.

An example will illustrate the point. A professor of British background was working in the U.S. when Argentina occupied the Falkland Islands. He had been away from England for a long time. He considered himself an intellectual and an objective analyst of international affairs. He had always liked Argentines. He had little concern for the islands and really did not care very much what happened to them. But somewhat to his surprise, he found himself reacting very emotionally to the occupation. *"No matter what the cost,"* he said to himself, *"we must* get the Argentines off those islands!"* He knew, however, that his response was irrational. His problem, then, as an intellectual interested in the full range of factors affecting the course of international events, was to try to locate the source of his intense feelings. How did he become so socialized in British values, sentiments, legend and identity that his reaction, multiplied by those of all his fellow citizens, made the retaking of the islands an unquestioned national imperative? It was not an easy question to answer.

This demonstrates, incidentally, why it is so difficult to produce mathematical models for simulating international scenarios. There is no easy way to quantify emotional charge or priority and rigidity of belief; yet among all the variables, these are often the most significant.

The more emotional intensity associated with a mindset, the more rigid that mindset becomes. An unshakable belief forces all perceptions to fall into line behind it. Thus, if one had to negotiate the future of the city of Jerusalem, one might be well advised to work from the premise that Palestinians and other Arab neighbors will always consider Israeli administration of that city totally unacceptable. Strong mindsets are just that—beliefs that are too deeply imbedded and too strongly supported by intense emotions to be easily changed.

12. *Will experience with differing social structures and the role behaviors that go with them affect perception of the issue?* Unfortunately, "social structure" is a fuzzy abstraction for most people; it resists becoming a practical conceptual tool. But for application across national societies, this question is a central one on the checklist. Social structure itself is an integral part of any cultural lens, and no two national societies are alike in this highly important dimension. As we noted in the last chapter, it is essential to examine how ingrained preconceptions regarding social status, privilege, pecking orders, wealth and poverty, and leadership affect outlooks on such things as politics, industrial relations, professional images, consumer aspirations, military command, and throughout all, person-to-person communication.

For example, if a socialist party were competing in an election, the voters' view from the vantage point of a rigidly structured society with a large and recognizable working class would be quite different from that of a society in which most people think of themselves as members of a mobile middle class—so would attitudes toward belonging to a labor union or reactions to advertising that associates a product with achievement and success. Likewise, government officials or corporation executives who feel themselves part of an achievement-oriented elite would see the world and their relations with other people differently from those in a society in which status is ascribed.

A follow-on question, equally useful in understanding cross-cultural communication problems, is how the cultural lens affects expectations regarding role behavior. How does culture provide a pattern of thinking which determines who can assume certain roles (lawyer, school teacher, politician or bureaucrat, for instance) and how the roles are played? What makes this worth special attention is that expected role behavior has two elements. One is the overt and obvious side that poses few problems cross-culturally. A position description will, for instance, tell you who qualifies to be a bureaucrat and what the duties are.

The other element, however, is much less obvious. Role behavior includes more subtle culturally-based expectations regarding the kind of people who can occupy positions, the style in which they must perform, and the way they should behave both on and off the job. To continue the example of the bureaucrat, culture determines what amount of authority is to be displayed or to what degree an egalitarian stance is to be taken, or what effect the bureaucrat's position has on his social status; does it, for instance, grant respect and deference or not? This theme will be developed further in the next chapter.

13. *What effect does experience with differing institutional forms, functions and operations have?* This parallels the last question, for institutions themselves are abstract entities with meaning and nuance derived from the many interconnected qualities of the larger cultural system. Therefore, a cultural lens colors expectations of an institution's actual operations. It is a matter of "role behavior," in effect, for institutions.

From a social-psychological perspective, institutions exist as pictures in the heads of the people who carry out institutionalized behavior. As discussed in the previous chapter, while institutions may be formalized in laws and regulations, their routine operation depends on the habitual behavior and thinking of participants and clients, and on the fact that much is taken for granted. What makes institutions hold together is the cultural and mental programming, the complex of shared knowledge, assumptions, beliefs, and expectations that go with banking or with a government bureaucracy, or whatever the institution in question.

The very mention of institutionalized activity—supervising office employees, campaigning for public office, teaching university classes—is a stimulus to set off all this programming. Therefore, the international dialogue becomes turgid if perspectives viewed through the cultural lenses or mindsets differ significantly. The temptation to project an interpretation onto the other's institutional behavior is automatic; and if the temptation is not controlled, the chance for error and misperception increases enormously.

Since much of international business is conducted at an institutional level, exploring how the larger culture and institutional system predisposes thinking about the performance of any given institution becomes a key consideration.

14. *To what extent are differing styles of logic and reasoning apparent? Are they reflected in language?* This is one of the more elusive elements to use in diagnosing the mindset interplay that surrounds an issue. As noted earlier, the question is whether cultures, augmented by their languages, tend to lead people to think and reason in distinctive ways, and if so, just what differences will be pertinent. We refer here to the discussion of the Whorfian hypothesis and related matters in the preceding chapter.

In simple terms we might say that if one feels comfortable interacting with counterparts because "they think just like us," then somehow one has to meet the problem when the counterpart does not think like "one of us." Earlier we referred to preferences for deductive versus inductive reasoning. If the tilt is toward deductive, then statements of principles, titles attached to items on conference agendas, or the "we hold these truths to be self-evident" style of reasoning would take priority in molding discussion and debate. If the style is more inductive, attention is directed first to facts, data, and details which, when accepted, allow discussion to move on to more general principles. The French tend to prefer the former, Americans the latter[3].

Styles of reasoning might also be affected by a culture's view toward categorization. For example, whereas one cultural group thinks in terms of opposites—good or bad, black or white, democratic or totalitarian—another might not make such clearcut delineations but rather think in terms of mixtures of some good, some bad, some black, some white. In this case, Americans prefer the former, people from the Orient the latter.

How far one can go in following this direction of inquiry will depend on one's preparation for delving into more abstruse aspects of thought and logic. At a minimum it is essential to recognize when patterns of thinking and logic are a factor in one's communication problem and to tentatively explore such contrasts as are evident. Again, much is to be gained by holding up for conscious examination the patterns of logic and reasoning associated with one's own culture and language.

Individual personality and group dynamics

15. *To what extent does the uniqueness of individual personality and experience need to be taken into account?* This question is intentionally presented near the end of the checklist because, as noted earlier, when mindsets are dealt with internationally, one needs to start first with overall group patterns of perception and reasoning that will help explain differing outlooks before focusing on individuals, important though the latter step may be.

International relations analysis has more typically focused on individuals such as a Winston Churchill or a Gandhi, or, at a more immediate level of international operations, on an opposite number whose name, face and background demand direct attention.

When working entirely within one society, the main context for individual variation is almost automatically understood. But cross-culturally, the underlying pattern changes. Now the question becomes not only how individuals are unique in terms of the norms to which I am accustomed in my society, but how they and their habits of thinking are unique in the context of their own society and culture.

A good sample from recent history of the interplay of these perceptions may be seen in the American reaction to Anwar Sadat. Americans tended to judge his personality much as they would have those of other Americans, finding it pleasing and a bit surprising that he was Egyptian, as though he had surmounted a handicap. He smoked a western-style pipe, after all. He had traveled, could tell jokes Americans could understand, and smiled at the right times. Above all, he seemed to be frank and open, pragmatic, and willing to consider compromise. But much more could have been understood about his outlooks and actions if his individuality had been seen in the context of Egyptian patterns of expected personality qualities where compromises, as in the Camp David accords, came near to disloyalty, and his kind of internationally urbane style suggested a lack of identity with the problems and concerns of the people back home. The outcome of his decisions and actions in Egypt would have been more accurately calculated by this approach, possibly even making his assassination less of a surprise.

16. *Are any special styles of group dynamics, information processing or decision making present?* In most institutional situations, people do not perceive and reason strictly on their own; they do it in groups—office staffs, country teams—through a chain of command. Thus, our diagnosis requires that we look into cross-cultural differences in decision making processes. Going no further than the idea of "group think" (discussed earlier) and applying it cross-culturally suggests the analytical task posed. Group think will operate quite differently in Japan, for instance, than in the United States.

What this question stresses is that observers avoid simply projecting onto a foreign decision-making process their own expectations regarding how and by whom decisions are arrived at, and look at group decision making from a perspective appropriate to the society. The task, again, is to look first for the overall or culturally established pattern in the way that groups reach decisions and then to such variations on the theme as are to be found in the setting of the moment.

Most of the preceding checklist questions come together, of course, at this nexus of international problem solving. Therefore, it is a convenient point at which to conclude.

The list has to be considered open-ended, but as it stands it should help the reader establish the range of considerations pertinent to the mindset factor in international practice. The list will now be applied in the following chapters to more specific areas of political and economic affairs.

Making Political Judgments in an International Setting

INTRODUCTION: THE MINDSET FACTOR IN POLITICAL AFFAIRS

We can expect that virtually all international operations will be affected by the way that governments govern and bureaucracies conduct their business. Consequently, everyone involved internationally has reason to be concerned with the way mindsets come into play in influencing the logic by which governments formulate policies, establish priorities, tax and regulate, and follow styles and practices which may or may not square with their formal declarations. Everyone becomes a political analyst in some degree, whether by studied intent or by default, as one projects a naive political common sense onto the international scene without really thinking much about it. In a foreign election, for example, it is all too easy to judge a candidate's electioneering tactics and appeals according to a scorecard from a different political culture.

Political observers from any country are culture bound to some extent, including officers of diplomatic services, journalists, and academic specialists. The ways in which this reduces the ability to cope in a foreign political environment are as varied as the subjects and working situations that come under the international relations umbrella. However, there are certain areas of governmental and bureaucratic affairs that especially invite application of mindset analysis as developed in the preceding chapters. A delineation of some of the more important of these will constitute the substance of this chapter. But first, we must re-emphasize the significance of psycho-cultural factors at the policy level of government-to-government relations where political judgments have such far-reaching consequences.

Consider how mindsets have to be diagnosed in the case of calculating "deterrence." Nuclear weapons are stockpiled on the psychological assumption that the *threat* of devastating destruction will be *perceived* by the other side as reason to resist its supposed inclination to start a war. Here is an instance in which the entire logic of the reasoning depends on psycho-cultural variables: What exactly is perceived as a "threat"? What level of destruction is "unacceptable"? Will threats be seen the same way by all who have nuclear capability, including doomsday decision makers in the Soviet Union, in the United States, in China or in Pakistan?

We might recall that in the Vietnam War, gross errors were made in calculating the level of "punishment" required to "force" the North Vietnamese to capitulate. At one point Secretary of State Dean Rusk told a television audience that he had personally underestimated the persistence and tenacity of the North Vietnamese, explaining that their estimated 700,000 casualties would be the equivalent of 10 million American casualties.[1] This is an interesting and highly culture bound way of equating a sense of casualty in the first place, and then of calculating its meaning against the Vietnamese sense of objective. A few years earlier, military leaders were assuring the American public that the damage of Hanoi's Tet offensive of early 1968 was "psychological, not real." This, as we now know, was the narrow outlook that ultimately led to a humiliating U.S. withdrawal. Even the *kind* of humiliation that was suffered was a function of an American mindset that made no provision for failing.

One of the major considerations in strategy sessions during that involvement was the American desire to maintain its "credibility." This preoccupation with credibility is in fact a rather constant American concern in policy making. Yet, credibility is a psychologically loaded term. In the final analysis, the credibility of U.S. actions is a function of some other society's outlook. In other words, being credible in one's own eyes does not necessarily equate with credibility based on another pattern of perception and reasoning—as we have already pointed out.

Defining aggressive intentions is another psychologically loaded factor in policy-related analysis, as is diagnosing benevolent intention. Judgments in these matters are the common element in a whole range of international war and peace calculations. One of the more frequently noted examples is MacArthur's misreading of

Chinese intentions during the Korean War when he persisted in driving to the Yalu River on the Chinese border. Argentine generals similarly misread British intentions, or at least likely reactions, when they attempted to take control of the Falkland Islands; they completely miscalculated British determination to fight rather than face the embarrassment of being pushed out. Persuasion in international diplomacy is also an exercise in calculating mindsets, from broadcasting propaganda to selecting negotiating positions, or from trying to win the "hearts and minds" of a nation to simple advertising.

It is clear, then, that international political astuteness at the government policy level must include an ability to judge motives and perceptions, to calculate the way an action will be understood and to predict the *actual consequences* of that action when psychological reality is taken into account. An amateurish and culture-bound performance has the odds against it. For example, at a press conference in 1982, then Secretary of State Alexander Haig was asked by a reporter why the U.S. was so upset about repression of political expression in Poland when it supported regimes in Turkey and other countries where similar conditions prevailed. The Secretary replied in some anger that the very implication of an equivalence "boggled the mind."[2] Presumably, statesmen and diplomats are people whose minds are not easily "boggled," particularly by differing points of view; in any case, his outright rejection of the possible significance of alternative perceptions suggested an ethnocentric mindset incompatible with international problem-solving skills.

The problem is to get culture bound strategists to recognize the crucial effect of unanticipated psychological determinants. Many who insist on "hard" and "realistic" approaches to international politics consider objective psycho-cultural calculations to be "soft" or "muddy" analysis, a predisposition for appeasement. In fact competent attention to the psycho-cultural dimension *is* the realistic approach, for it is the approach by which judgments can be based on real cause-and-effect relationships rather than on vague and superficial dependence on hunches and unexamined assumptions. The objective, after all, is to accurately calculate consequences. This lesson had not been learned by the activists on President Reagan's National Security Council staff in 1986 when they undertook the infamous arms for hostages deal with Iran.

These amateurs who made Americans feel good because of their hard-line, get-things-done approach and their impatience with stodgy bureaucratic decision making were in fact the ones who were soft and muddy in their judgments. But it took Congressional hearings to make that clear. Even so, immediately thereafter and with little more "hard" calculation of the psychologically volatile Iran situation, the Reagan Administration dispatched naval forces to the Persian Gulf to escort Kuwaiti oil tankers through the jaws of the Iran-Iraq war

Interestingly, decision makers who will forthrightly base international actions on a naive, culture bound, common-sense approach would never personally consider submitting their medical problems to a doctor who diagnosed by folk belief, nor would they calculate a real estate deal or stock option without seeking the best judgment possible of all the factors, including the psychological, which determine value and performance.

However, most people concerned with international affairs do not participate in high-level government deliberations; most occasions for making political judgments are more routine. The problem more typically involves the straightforward assessment of political processes and governmental performance within a country that is foreign to the observer. At the least, one can always expect to have to deal with foreign government officials if only to get a visa or conform to local laws and regulations. Therefore, let us now turn to several of the more specific facets of governmental and bureaucratic affairs that typically and routinely pose mindset problems.

PROJECTING ASSUMPTIONS AS TO HOW GOVERNMENT OUGHT TO WORK

The key word here is "ought." Most people undertaking international responsibilities will not have studied comparative government extensively enough to quickly tune their antennae to the underlying assumptions and logic by which governmental institutions in the country to which they have been assigned operate. They will instead carry in their cultural baggage a sense of how governmental matters *should* be handled, based solely on the sociopolitical conditioning they received at home. Thus, that which is most foreign may not be the relatively easily observed differences in regulations and procedures, but the ways of thinking behind them—the ideas and assumptions that supply both ordinary citizens and government officials with an on-going sense of standard operating procedures. A parliament, for instance, differs from the U.S. Congress in more than the style of legislative proceedings or rules by which a prime minister exercises authority. It also differs in the sense government officials have of how people are expected to relate to each other, in the sense they have of parliamentary ethics, of timing, or of what actually can be done. Or a police department is not "foreign" simply in the laws it enforces or in its bureaucratic ways of processing wrongdoers. It may operate with a differing set of expectations regarding its authority, who controls it (perhaps the Ministry of Interior), or the nature of its ongoing relationship with the public. Its actions may be based on different underlying assumptions: Is one presumed to be innocent until proven guilty or guilty unless proven innocent? In some countries it is a good idea to flee the scene of an automobile accident even if you are sure you are not responsible; otherwise, you may be held in jail until innocence is certified by proper authority.

Hence, the possibility of misperception for the outside observer is not so much a matter of failing to recognize foreign customs of government that are easily described in rules and regulations, but of the inability to capture the mindsets that go with those rules and procedures. Unfortunately, if one asks foreign colleagues to explain the underlying philosophy and fundamental assumptions that apply to the way their government functions, the chances are that the answer, even if the question is taken seriously, will be a confusion of schoolbook pronouncements and unstudied rationalizations. Most people do not routinely dwell on the way that they are programmed to think about government and its operations. It is not necessary; the logic of government is taken for granted. Yet, even in dealing with such near cousins as the British, the mindset difference is great enough that socialized medicine, the propriety of a labor party, or large expenditures to support a royal family confront Americans with a degree of "foreign" political mentality. Outsiders cannot rely on their political judgments in any other country without somehow picking up the nuances of its political culture, picking up the subtle feeling *they* have of how things *ought* to be done.

Assumptions differ, for instance, as to how much authority a government should exercise. One wonders, from an American perspective, how Russian citizens tolerate the invasion of government into so many aspects of daily life and personal affairs. But for Russians it may not be an entirely unwelcomed intrusion. Studies indicate that Russian political culture, even before the Communist system was put in place, sanctioned such practices. Long before the Communists came to power, Russians, much more than Americans, were inclined to see the average citizen as more given to excesses and as less likely to exercise self-control. Government, therefore, was expected to restrain people, to curb the impulses which undermined group well-being. Government was expected to attend to the citizen's needs and in turn to provide guidance, check performance, and demand obedience. It was considered oppressive not when it fulfilled this more authoritative role, but when it acted in ways that were impersonal, capricious, unjust, or abusive of its authority to the detriment of the communal group or of Russian society.[3] Because this seems to go against "human nature" to people socialized in an American political culture, it is unlikely that Americans could make a sound judgment of governmental and bureaucratic actions in the USSR without exploring differences in what seems "natural" in governmental structures and operations.

Japanese expectations as to "natural" government functions are still different. Authority operates in a particularly unfamiliar psychological context, one in which a sense of mutual obligation, enjoying an almost religious sanction and existing in an extremely homogeneous society, holds the system together. Government there is infused with a Japanese sense of ethnic identity, of which the Emperor has traditionally served as a symbol. Officials pursue their functions with codes of honor and a sense of responsibility that make sense only within the Japanese system.

Several kinds of contrasting "deep culture" assumptions typically present problems. Perhaps the most important derives from the question: Does the government govern primarily in the interest of the individual (and for the individual's welfare) or in the interest of the group—that is, the interest of the society at large? This question can rarely be given an "either-or" answer relative to any specific country, but contrasts in value emphasis are obvious. The United States stands near one end of the spectrum, with the individual and individual opportunity, freedom of expression, and even pursuit of individual "happiness" being the central objectives. Only as a last resort may the law, normally designed to preserve individual rights, be used to hem people in, if necessary, to protect the rights of other individuals or the national interest. Wartime restrictions have been placed on individual liberties but are seen as exceptions to be abandoned as soon as possible. Politics in many cases becomes a debate over the degree to which individual freedom must necessarily be limited.

As noted above, more traditional societies, along with governments in the Communist mold, turn the objective around. It is the group and its well-being that come first—to which the individual must conform. It is a good government that does the right thing for the collective citizenry and keeps the deviant and disruptive individual in line. Government is supposed to think in terms of group and collective objectives. Such is not a society of unlimited opportunity for the individual, for that would be seen as being achieved at the expense of the group. In fact, most of the world finds these implicit assumptions about government more congenial to their thinking than would most Americans. The United States is probably somewhat unique in the degree to which a governmental and even economic system cater so heavily to individual choice.

In large part, gut-level expectations regarding the ways that government should operate are functions of the social structure of the country in question. Again, the United States, with its particular kind of democratic governmental system, occupies one end of a spectrum, where society is essentially open or middle class. At the other end stands the society with a tightly structured class system. American society is fluid; mobility is expected (even though deriving the benefits of social mobility is not always easy). Hence, government is preoccupied with the kind of regulation that protects this mobility, the social flux, the middle-class life. Governments in more tightly structured societies with traditional governing classes operate on different expectations. The social segment that gets ahead is the one that can control government; social *groups* compete for power. As the power of elites and oligarchies is broken, labor as a segment of society tends to become a stronger political force. The *descamisados*—the shirtless ones—of Argentina became a forceful political group during the Peron era. Racial and ethnic groups striving for identity may further complicate matters. What is seen with alarm in the U.S. as "fragmentation politics" is the normal condition of government in many countries. That is, the political process is more a contest among *segments* of the social structure.

Perceptions of government can also differ as to its proper role: as guardian of a given social order or tradition on the one hand, as an instrument of change and modernization on the other (as it is in many developing countries). If a government is revolutionary in origin, charismatic in leadership, and tuned to current aspirations, the mandate, both spoken and deeply felt, is to make large changes in the society and its conditions, and to do it quickly. Government may then be caught in between as it tries to decide what accommodation to make to modernization and what traditional ways should be preserved. Such a situation lends itself to great inconsistency because the supporting beliefs and expectations of the society at large are themselves inconsistent. This lack of supporting shared programming as to what government ought to be about poses great difficulties for both the society and for outside observers, especially those from the industrialized world as they try to diagnose the political process.

Some divergence exists in what publics expect of their governments: whether the government should stand relatively alone in running the country or whether other institutions should share the function. The existence of strong local governments, religious organizations, community or village institutions, etc., affect public outlooks on how all-pervading a central government's power should be. While the proper reach of the federal government is a source of continuing debate in the United States, it would be less of a debate in countries where a highly centralized government is the tradition; the central government would prevail.

For example, any foreign observer used to centralized planning would have had a difficult time understanding the debate in the state of Indiana in the early days of federal funding for interstate highways. Hoosiers questioned whether these funds should be accepted at all because they felt that it might give the federal government intolerable influence over Indiana's right to conduct its own affairs.

Further, there are contrasting assumptions regarding the degree of rigidity or uniformity with which laws should be enforced. Should government be stern and authoritarian in style, precise in the execution of its regulations, as is the tendency in

Germany, or is it expected to be more understanding, compliant, ready to make exceptions, as in the Philippines (even during the martial law days)? While this seems like a minor point in standard international political analysis, it is a significant issue for anyone working within a foreign governmental system.

In sum, what is required is the ability to move from one's initial built-in sense of how government *ought* to work to an understanding of how a newly-encountered government actually *does* work. But that is not enough. To complete the process one must attempt to understand *why* a government works as it does, based on the expectations of the governed as to how it ought to work.

ANTICIPATING THE PUBLIC'S SENSE OF HOW POLITICAL PROCESSES OUGHT TO WORK

Few subjects will be so central to ordinary discussion overseas as the political process—or, more simply, "politics." In many countries it is the national sport. And it is hard to follow the game without knowing the rules, which involves more than just the rules themselves. "Political culture" is thus more than an abstract term; it is, in fact, the practical key to understanding and anticipating not only how the political system works but how people think it *ought* to work.

One of the more salient examples of the way that perception of proper politics is "programmed" is the American preoccupation with voting. They project this programming overseas. Thus, almost any kind of government can gain control or any program action be embarked upon and have an aura of rightfulness in American eyes if there has been a vote on the matter. Indeed, voting is central to the democratic process, but it has become something of an all-pervading staple in the American mindset in the perception of both domestic and foreign political affairs. It matters surprisingly little how the voting in question was conducted, how the issue was presented, or how small the turnout was. If the opportunity for a fair vote was part of the process, the result has respectability; it is given a seal of acceptance, often to the point that an otherwise intolerable policy or set of officials can be lived with.

Conversely, evidence of an unfair vote immediately destroys legitimacy in American eyes, a factor of central importance in the events that led to the exit of President Marcos from the Philippines in 1986. Similarly, a vote simply to approve or disapprove an action which is already a fait accompli is seen by Americans as manipulation, a sham. Parenthetically, it might be noted that this outlook reaches political absurdity in the United Nations General Assembly where, in a one-nation-one-vote forum, a vote by the United States vies for influence in world affairs on more or less equal terms with those of the Maldive Islands and Grenada. The dilemma is that habits of perception force American participants to see a positive process at work in the U.N. General Assembly, when the practical intellect suggests an element of artificiality in it all.

Hence, in exploring mindsets that go with the political culture in which one is working, the first question to ask might be: by what idea patterns is the *legitimacy* of a political process defined? What gives a public the comfortable feeling that the way that decisions are reached and leaders are chosen is "right"? We have said that in the United States there is an aura of rightness—even to the losers— if people vote among alternatives. This extends even to the point that public opinion polling is becoming part of the political process in the United States, almost as a substitute for a referendum. Poll results sanction or censure an action. But this involves a logic that is not necessarily shared by other political cultures, even in areas where the impulse to modernize has led to the adoption of an elective form of government in the hope that competence in the modernization process will follow. Too often the sense of legitimacy that supposedly goes with voting and democratic elections takes longer to develop than the imported political structures.

The reason is that the patterns of thinking behind political processes are not easily duplicated. For example, an essential concept that has to go with the voting process is the notion of "fair play"—a peculiarly English word (noted in Chapter II) not found in any other language except as an adoption, as in the French "le fer ple." When this value orientation is not part of the public mindset, the consequences of an election can be devastating. Winning and losing are seen very differently. Defeat is not easily accepted; being in opposition really *is* opposition.

Or consider positive and negative views of "compromise," which is also related to legitimacy in the political process. To the American, the fact of having arrived at a compromise gives a degree of sanction per se. This is a prominent American-British pattern of logic, which in such pure form appears in the political affairs of few other countries. Even when adopted as part of the cosmopolitan culture of international business, the notion of compromise is not equally comfortable to all users. Even a concept such as "public interest" is subject to great variation interculturally; in some cases it has no meaning at all.

Perhaps the greatest cross-cultural task is posed when a Westerner has to understand and cope with actions deriving their legitimacy from political assumptions far removed from the accepted Western mold. In what way is a guerilla movement legitimate in the minds of those participating in it or of those who see it as a more or less reasonable and expected part of their political reality? Or still more difficult for the Judeo-Christian mind is terrorism as an instrument of politics. The rationalizations on which terrorism is based seem to border on the insane or at least on the criminal, as viewed from mainstream Western conceptions of legitimacy. Yet to those involved, Palestinians, for example, there is *some* pattern of thought by which terrorism or more complex insurgent movements are seen as justified; and these idea patterns relate to the most basic and emotionally laden aspects of life and death, martyrdom, loyalty, enmity, retribution, etc., as well as warfare conducted by unconventional methods. However abnormal this behavior is—even if one believes it verges on the definably insane—it stems from a mindset that requires careful analytical attention if it is to be understood and its consequences anticipated or predicted. Miscalculating or dismissing behavior as insane or irrational does not solve real international problems, as the Iran hostage crisis so clearly illustrated.

A more common, but equally foreign, source of legitimacy in some political cultures is, of course, religion. Islamic fundamentalism in Iran is a prime example. This is somewhat different from the way religion appears as a political factor in Northern Ireland, Poland, or even the United States. Islam is itself a kind of system of government with a value system and a philosophy by which society is structured.

Formal ideologies are also sources of legitimacy and as such merit serious psycho-cultural analysis. Their journey toward a genuine public sense of legitimacy, however, is a long one, for ideologies start out as mind *constructs* championed by ideological leaders, rather than popular mindsets. They then have to become mindsets among the populace at large in order to serve a legitimizing function. This explains the authoritarian tactics frequently employed by governments that come to power in an ideologically-based revolution. In Sandinista Nicaragua people even talked of aligning themselves with "the process"—an interesting study in changing political culture.

PROJECTING ASSUMPTIONS AS TO HOW PUBLIC OFFICIALS OUGHT TO PLAY THEIR ROLES.

In overseas operations errors in dealing with local officials and bureaucrats often arise because outsiders' expectations do not match local expectations regarding the kind of behavior, responsibility, sense of duty, power to act, or identification with the public interest that goes with the official position. The discrepancy between projected expectations and actual behavior sets off a chain of misinterpretations related to competence and motives that not only results in mistakes in working in the system, but usually in dysfunctional emotional reactions as well. When the way an official role is played is too far from one's experience and expectations, it is easy to assume that there is something wrong with the official. Some of the most heated reactions from world travelers is directed at officers and clerks in the Indian bureaucracy, where bureaucratic behavior simply as an end in itself seems to have come to full flower!

Perhaps one of the more extreme problems presented in analyzing role behavior at the chief-of-state level has been that posed by Libya's Colonel Muammar Kadaffi during tense periods in the mid-1980s. By all Western standards, he has appeared to be an erratic and dangerously irresponsible personality, perhaps insane. Yet, because of his pretentions to leadership in the Arab world, and especially because of his part in aiding and abetting terrorists, his role and behavior had to be understood if policies to contain his excesses were to be successful. In some respects his style was near the fringes of acceptable behavior in traditional Middle Eastern society, except that in the Middle East, as in other areas experiencing rapid political change and social dislocation, the role of a charismatic leader allows considerable nonconformity, as was demonstrated by Egypt's late Gamal Abdul Nasser, whom Kadaffi emulated. Thus, it was difficult for outsiders to determine the degree to which Kadaffi's flamboyant and extravagant behavior was an asset or a liability in his own society and in the Middle East as a whole, or to calculate how fragile his position might be. Perhaps his stature was even increased by the degree to which the West overreacted, taking him more seriously than necessary.[4] In any case, it was difficult to know what actions against him would have the effect of discrediting him in his own political realm.

One of the aspects of Kadaffi's behavior that has been especially hard to interpret has been his grandiose rhetoric. Experts tell us rhetorical exaggeration is an art form among Middle Eastern leaders and is recognized as such. When a leader says that he intends to do something, it does not necessarily follow that he really means to do it. It may be recalled that this kind of verbal license caused trouble even among the Arab nations themselves during the 1967 war with Israel. It was expected that statements made among the Arab allies regarding damage inflicted and sustained would be exaggerated or minimized—but by how much? In consequence, when Egyptian forces were being driven back, Syrian and Jordanian strategists were unable to establish the real situation from Egyptian accounts, compounding the overall problem of coordination.

Thus the dilemma for decision makers. When the U.S. elected to challenge Kadaffi by naval confrontation in the Gulf of Sidra and by air raids on Tripoli and Benghazi in retaliation for his support of terrorists, calculating the actual effect of the raids would have depended heavily on an accurate diagnosis of Kadaffi's role and status in his own culture and the political consequences for him which would result from the military confrontation.

On the other hand, the foreign official who must make political estimates of American behavior also faces role behavior interpretation problems. U.S. Foreign Service Officers repeatedly find themselves trying to assure host government officials that an outspoken U.S. senator or congressman is *not* speaking officially when he makes a public statement about the country in question. The bounds of customary congressional behavior are complex enough even within the United States; they become nearly impossible to explain in areas where local role behavior is substantially different. The ease with which people wrongly attribute motive is all too apparent to the American diplomat who has to do the explaining!

Political analysis deals rather constantly, of course, with authority—who has it, why, and for what use? This is an across-the-board concern in overseas operations. It poses problems for Peace Corps volunteers working with a town mayor or local education official as well as for the corporation executive interpreting promises of a tax concession or for a diplomat analyzing positions taken by cabinet officers.

In examining the way official role behavior varies from one political culture to another, it may be helpful to recall the typology suggested by Max Weber for analyzing bureaucratic authority.[5] Weber posed three fundamental modes of authority: *traditional, legal-rational,* and *charismatic.* Like all analytical models, these require mixing and modifying in application, but they serve well to suggest a practical line of inquiry in field situations and are worth some exploration here as examples of the kinds of mindsets that lie behind role behavior.

Traditional authority depends on who you are. This kind of thinking is still very strong in many places, even in areas that appear to be largely modernized. The Middle East, Latin America, and parts of Asia offer repeated examples. In this mode, officials exercise authority not simply by the powers of the office they occupy, but also by the personal qualities they bring to the office. Their ascribed status, elite position, family, character, personal relations with other officials (either by family connection or personal friendship or trust) provide an implicit authority that cannot be gained simply by passing a civil service examination or being selected according to technical qualifications. A House of Lords in Britain survives from a more traditional period in British history. In Latin America this kind of traditionalism is reflected in the political salience of the "public man" image, as discussed earlier. In Saudi Arabia it is embodied in the royal family.

In these cases, those who would understand how government works need to pay careful attention to: who the incumbent is, who he is related to, what society-honored features of personality are exhibited, what the pattern of personal obligations is (or, conversely, who the incumbent's enemies are), where breaks in personal relationships occur, and what kind of behavior undermines the authority image. It is a situation in which the incumbent dignifies the position, not the other way around. This role calls for respect and deference to be accorded to the person, not the office. Decisions are made more as projections of person and a need to maintain personal relationships in the authority system, less on technical law or argument.

Most Westerners who deal with government and management are more accustomed to the *legal-rational* basis for authority. It comes with the position and gives the incumbent an aura of authority that would not be present otherwise. Uniqueness of individual personality is downplayed, chain of command is specified, and the range of responsibility is spelled out in a job description. The incumbent qualifies for the position, enhances authority by competent performance, and is advanced by experience and merit. When the incumbent leaves the office at the end of the day, the authority remains behind. Equipment is marked "for official use only," a contradiction in terms in traditional systems. Hiring relatives appears to be an abuse of authority, a threat to public confidence that the competence of the officers and the integrity of the office will be sustained.

The observer who must decipher authority in such a system looks much more closely to the institutions themselves and the way they are organized, to the way new incumbents are trained or prepared for their duties, to laws and regulations. One attempts to persuade officials in such a system by reasoned argument and reference to regulations and accepted operating procedure. When a service is desired, one seeks the *office* that is supposed to perform that service, not the key individual who is able to see that it is done.

Finally, authority can be based on the incumbent's *charismatic* qualities. This is the patriot, the ideological hero, the one who embodies the beliefs, emotions and aspirations of a movement, or the one who has earned his credentials and gained a personal mystique in the heat of the political struggle. This is authority gained regardless of traditional standards or technical qualifications. Zeal and sacrifice count more. This basis for authority may appear somewhat evanescent and over time may require the addition of traditional or legal-rational ingredients. Yet, charismatic leadership can still be enthusiastically embraced by society, or at least by that part of the society that supports the ideal the incumbent represents.

Confronted with this pattern of authority, the analyst must look carefully at the beliefs, emotions, experiences, and aspirations which set the stage for charismatic solutions to political matters. One must be wary of overly rational or logical explanations of the role behavior of a Fidel Castro, Adolph Hitler, Gandhi, or perhaps even a Dwight Eisenhower.

Obviously, these three patterns of authority rarely exist in pure form, and, indeed, sociologists point to many other role considerations. Age gives authority in the Orient; advanced academic degrees add clout to an incumbent's personal authority in India; demonstrated achievement or specialization helps make one an authority figure in the United States. Ascertaining such aspects of political culture can pay dividends for the practitioner who attempts to anticipate how an official will perceive issues and events and, most especially, choose his action in a given situation.

It should also be obvious that there is a reverse side to this coin: the status and role expectations for those who are the *clients* in governmental and bureaucratic affairs. Role patterns tend to come in pairs—government official on the one hand and, in this case, the person seeking official services on the other. Applying Weber's authority models, if the authority were traditional, it would make a difference *who* the client is, who the client is connected to. In the case of legal-rational authority, this would not be so important, but having the technical details in place would be. If the authority were charismatic, what the client believes, and how enthusiastically, might make the difference.

LAW AS A PATTERN OF POLITICAL AND SOCIAL PERCEPTION

Political judgments often involve problems which are essentially legal. This brings up the relationship between culture and law and suggests that if one is prepared to read between the lines as one deals with law in a foreign setting, the payoff will be an insight into the moral and philosophical outlooks of the society. In a sense, law consists of mindsets set in concrete.

On the surface, law appears to be the instrument for regulating and enforcing behavior; people necessarily comply to avoid punishment. Actually, in most systems, law is more a codification of what the society *already believes and values,* a codification of the mindsets that are at work as related to commercial dealings, marriage, settling conflicts, or whatever. Therefore, compliance with the law comes naturally; it is based more on sharing the mindset than on fearing the sanction.

Consequently, for our purposes here, much is to be gained by seeking out the patterns of thinking behind the law by examining legal philosophy and built-in conceptions of the good society and moral behavior. The importance of this kind of analysis is recognized in such subdisciplines as the sociology of law and the anthropology of law. The tight relationship between law and culture is often cited as the principal cause of difficulty in imposing new laws that do not mesh with the culture or in enforcing old laws based on values that have changed over time. It also explains why developing effective international law is so difficult; the basis in a common culture or shared mindsets is not there.

If law reflects mindsets, a useful line of inquiry is presented. Here are a number of questions which seem especially relevant.

• As one encounters the established legal codes of a given country, *what does the society appear to assume about the proper function of government and of political processes, about rights and duties, moral and immoral behavior, and the ideal society?* How can one explain local laws as being logical for the society and culture in question? For example, what could a foreign observer conclude about American values and assumptions by considering the mindsets behind the jury system as contrasted with other systems where guilt in criminal cases is determined by judges. Why has divorce become legal in Italy, but not Ireland—both Catholic countries? Is it a different Catholic culture?

• *What can be learned about the moral basis of a government when laws are not consistent with actual practices?* In rapidly changing political systems, such as those found in many nations which were once colonies or which are governed under newly imposed ideologies, the mindsets and values supporting law are in flux. In what ways do traditional beliefs combine with modern legal and political innovations? Note that this was a very relevant question when a democratic constitution was imposed on Japan at the end of World War II, and is now in the modernizing Middle East where, in opposition to the fundamentalists, traditional Islamic legal ideas are being modified, or at least challenged, to accommodate new political and governmental imperatives. In the latter case the conflict in ideas frequently translates into violence. Often in observing the effort to compromise old and new laws, one can better appreciate the fundamental clash over the moral basis for making a wider range of governmental decisions, such as who will pay taxes, who gets governmental services, or what use will be made of public office.

Actually, the inter-relationship between ideology and the mindsets which underlie the law is of special interest in this context, especially as so many people working internationally have to judge whether their counterparts are operating within the logic of a formal ideology or on the basis of on-going culture. Or, they need to judge how an adopted or imposed ideology is modified by pre-existing culture. China is a dramatic example. When are the Chinese Chinese? When they are Communists? Or when, as it seems today, they are following traditional Chinese entrepreneurial instincts? Or, which Spaniards still think in terms of the ideology of the Franco era and which in terms of democratic socialism—or in what mix?

When a new ideology becomes the basis of law during revolutionary change, the law is *intended* to mold new mindsets. In making political judgments, the problem posed for the outside observer is: Where do matters stand? To what extent are the patterns of thinking that go with the new ideology actually the operative basis for perceiving and reasoning on the part of the people with whom one must deal? We noted above the implications of this problem for "legitimacy" questions.

The complication that becomes especially difficult yet important in dealing with legal procedures in a foreign country is the existence of unwritten law, or of customs for sidestepping the law—patterned immorality and illegality, if you will. Government and law do not always operate by the formal rules, and the deviations, even though informally structured and understood by those who live in the country, are not easily anticipated and understood by outsiders. Even in thievery and corruption, certain informal norms often apply.

I recall the complaint of a Foreign Service Officer going through an area study seminar before departure for a new overseas assignment. The basic textbook-like material presented on his country of destination and its culture was all well and good, he thought, but he could get that on his own. He wanted something more practical. Now if someone could explain ahead of time the customary ways by which his new hosts were likely to try to "do the stranger in"—that would be useful!

In short, the subtle art of tuning in to the mindsets that sanction avoiding or manipulating law becomes a very useful asset for making high quality judgments which will hold up in the actual course of events. The payoff comes in meeting problems large and small. In Mexico City it used to be conventional wisdom that if one lost one's wallet to a pickpocket, it was a good idea to go to the post office to retrieve it. It was customary for pickpockets, who were decent chaps, after all, to remove usable currency and then toss the wallet with all its other contents, such as drivers license, into a mail box. A considerable convenience for the victim. And in the corporate world, it is conventional wisdom in many places to engage the services of a local "lawyer" to "expedite" the processing of official documents, for such a person understands what is needed beyond the technical requirements of the law: the function of gifts, flattery, and reciprocal favors to move things through a bureaucratic mill. A stranger in the United States would have trouble following American thinking about exceeding posted highway speeds. Apparently one breaks the law, but by how much? Americans would be outraged to get a ticket for going two miles over the speed limit. But somewhere between five and ten miles beyond the limit we sense that illegal speed is really illegal. The wonderful world of mindsets!

• *To whom do laws and regulations apply* in a given country, and in what situations? Even when laws are well stipulated and codified, equality before the law and universal application get mixed up with other assumptions regarding social structure and the relationship of the individual to the law. The very idea of being elite in some societies may mean being above the law. Social connections with influential people or customs of reciprocity may be the culture's way of obtaining the necessary personal intervention to escape legal machinery. Or, especially in traditional societies, the law can be seen as an instrument of power and advantage for those who have access to it. Government may be used and law applied or not as a matter of personal choice by those in power. In such systems, graft and corruption have a different meaning.[6]

The point is that such manipulation of the law can be part of public expectations. Even those who criticize the abuse of power by their countrymen would expect themselves to abuse it if they were in a position to do so. I recall a public speech given in the Southern Philippines in the pre-Marcos era which addressed the rather endemic public preoccupation with graft and corruption—an area of official behavior where basic conceptions of law and authority were inconsistent with the ideal that had been only partly implanted in the public mind during the U.S. administration of the Islands. A reformist Congressman at the podium charged that his audience was *not* against graft and corruption. They were just disappointed that there was not enough to go around.

In so-called civic cultures, laws and regulations may be valued for the essential order they provide in public affairs. They are expected to apply universally. Individuals feel a vested interest in knowing everyone adheres to them, including themselves. But this theme has variations. On the one hand, Germans, who appreciate orderliness, clear instruction and efficiency, are particularly noted for solving problems by promulgating regulations. Americans, on the other hand, tend to view regulatory laws as instrumentalities, to be used and manipulated in solving problems. It has been argued that in the Hispanic world, people view law as an expression of an ideal, almost a work of art, which may be admired and appreciated but which does not necessarily apply to them personally. There was a cartoon in Spain which won an award for best expressing Spanish national character. It depicted a small boy urinating in the dust and spelling with the stream "Viva Yo"—Long Live Me! This is not the kind of ego that submits graciously to impersonal legal precepts.[7]

• Then a key question to consider is that which would be proposed by an anthropologist: If law does not serve to control behavior, *what other institutions or mental programming will actually serve as the controlling force for sanctioning or censoring behavior* or for defining what is right and wrong in a given society? In what way does the value system of the culture formulate an ethic which, when shared by the society and internalized by individuals, functions to control behavior, irrespective of law? In North America and Northern Europe, culture tends, quite aside from law, to supply a *sin-and-guilt* control mechanism based in part on religious views embodied with particular clarity in the Protestant ethic and in Calvinist preaching. The expected function of religion, in this case, is to define right and wrong, to set the rules for moral and ethical behavior. Law in these areas has been more or less consistent with religious doctrine.

In Southern Europe, the Middle East, and Latin America, on the other hand, *shame* tends to be the control mechanism of choice, with one's relationship to other people and to the group the context for determining acceptable behavior. Ethics are thus more related to the situation and who is involved. In these areas religion is relied on less for its ethical prescriptions.

In the Orient the same motif is seen in ideas of "face," honor, dignity, and obligation, all strong agents for controlling behavior, irrespective of law. In Hindu and Buddhist societies religious systems do play an important role in regulating behavior, but how they do so differs markedly from the way Protestantism affects behavior in Europe and America. There, modern laws and regulations, especially Western law, constitute a superimposed system not necessarily sanctioned by pre-existing culture and society.

THE IMAGE FACTOR IN INTERNATIONAL POLITICS AND OFFICIAL BEHAVIOR

As stated earlier, it is not so much what happens as what people think is happening that counts, both in international affairs in general and in more mundane administrative affairs. The stage for what people, including government officials and bureaucrats, think is happening is set in large part by national self-images and images of the other nation or culture, that is, by what they have come to expect of themselves and of others. In the best circumstances, such as in working with cosmopolitan counterparts, these images may be reliable because of shared experiences or clear role definitions. There is usually some distortion, however, in the case of public images as they affect international processes—often wild distortions. Realistic political judgments simply cannot be made without taking the image factor into studied consideration and examining its effect.

Images have come to be recognized for their significance in international relations.[8] And government policy makers normally take them into account. The manipulation of images is, for example, the concern of propaganda. The United States Information Agency tries to promote better images of the United States, which means, of course, images of America in line with the way we see ourselves. Corporations are also concerned with their image abroad and usually set aside a budget for advertising or for supporting local charities or otherwise tending to public impressions. Both scholars and policy makers understand, if often imprecisely, that the actual consequences of a given policy initiative or overseas program will be determined not only by that policy's logic as understood in diplomatic circles or by the skill used in presenting and executing it, but also by the images held by the target populace of the country (or organization) identified with the policy or program.

But perhaps even more important to examine are national self-images. We will dwell on this subject at some length because it constitutes so basic a psychological factor in determining a nation's international behavior and the behavior of its official representatives.

A confident self-image based on a sense of moral, economic or military *superiority* (or all three) has frequently been a powerful factor in determining a nation's style of international behavior. The British Empire depended on it. For centuries the Chinese view of the world had its basis in an image of China as the Central Kingdom, the boundaries of which separated civilized society from that of the barbarian. Much of the U.S. approach to world affairs is rooted in the images Americans have of themselves as having created a successful democratic political system and as possessing a special genius for problem solving, all of which has tended to give them a sense of international mission. Thus, the self-satisfaction Americans take in what they consider the altruistic aspects of such U.S. initiatives as the Marshall Plan and the Alliance for Progress, or simply in intervening in the affairs of other countries or serving as consultants and advisors abroad.

Opposed to this is the *dependent* self-image. This is an entirely different lens for viewing world events and for following the policies and actions of the superpowers. It is the view of the bystander rather than the actor, of the supplicant rather than the manipulator, of the one who reacts to events rather than causes them. It is the view of the nation that can see strength only in union or blocs, for which the United Nations General Assembly is a welcomed forum. Whereas the superpower identifies its interests with the larger scene in which international affairs are acted out, the smaller countries are more likely to think in terms of repercussions in their countries alone. At the least, it is difficult for the dependent countries to identify with the interests of the larger powers in the way those powers might wish or expect. It is understandable then when the Third World turns deaf ears to the priority concerns in world affairs held dear by the larger nations, even when these concerns—protecting the environment, for instance, or conserving energy resources—are global in scope and transcend the self-interest of any one nation or group of nations.

The United States probably carries a liability simply because of its size, as was apparent in the reaction to U.S. actions in Vietnam. Observers from neutral countries, even those who were inclined to agree with American intentions, expressed the feeling that the game was unfair. Sympathy tended to be extended to North Vietnam as the small boy on the street attacked by the bully with all the expensive equipment and big bombs. Americans themselves tend to favor the underdog, but prefer to believe that in international affairs they are championing the cause of the world's underdogs rather than being themselves the underdog's problem. But such "misinterpretation" of U.S. intentions cannot simply be dismissed as irrational. Iranians probably really did think the U.S. was the overpowering "big Satan"; for them this mindset was hard reality. Many Filipinos really have seen the U.S. as an uncertain benefactor; they have the sense that their country has been ejected from a special paternalistic relationship which at one time had been comfortable.

Few countries take their dependency relationships to be the natural order of things except perhaps in fatalistic resignation. An exception would seem to have been the case of Japan during at least the first two decades following World War II. The Japanese apparently had relatively little difficulty adjusting to the fact that the U.S. was the superior power because they, the Japanese, were able to extend to the international arena their cultural view of hierarchy and place. The war established what the superior-dependent status was; this at least supplied the security of a known position. It might be argued that the Japanese did not necessarily find such a relationship undesirable or undignified. In personal relationships the *amae* concept is consistent with this outlook, as in the case when a student is dependent on a teacher, or a child on its parents, or an employee on an employer. Consequently, the benevolent dominance of the Americans after the war seemed the proper role of the superior in the *amae* relationship, and the Japanese responded accordingly. This is changing, of course, as the power relationship itself changes. The psychological stance is, however, in direct contrast to that of the Mexicans, whose hypersensitivity to the affront to dignity posed by U.S. power always has to be considered in U.S.-Mexican relations.

In the Third World, then, larger powers are often viewed as the agents responsible for the difficulties of underdevelopment. It is they who monopolize natural resources and manipulate international economic processes to their advantage. Favors or assistance obtained from a big power, therefore, may not be seen as gifts requiring gratitude or reciprocity, but as due recompense or a regaining of what was rightfully theirs in the first place. I recall the case of a typewriter stolen from a Peace Corps office during a student demonstration in Bolivia. It was openly being used in an office in the university student center. When an intermediary challenged these students on the use of stolen property, they explained it was not stolen, but repatriated. The same feeling, or a cousin to it, figures into the attitudes which sustain the demand for a "New World Economic Order."

Even in disaster situations, these kinds of feelings can come into play. India has paid dearly for wheat from the Soviet Union rather than be the recipient of still more relief supplies from the United States. Until the major 1985 earthquake, Mexico refused most forms of foreign public assistance.

As might be expected, dependency resentment often arises from perceptions of having been violated. A good example is seen in the charge other countries level at the U.S. of being manipulated by the Central Intelligence Agency and in the anxiety and sensitivity generated regarding the Agency's activities. In U.S. political circles, the importance of this concern as a serious basis for perceiving U.S. intentions has rarely been carefully analyzed and taken fully into account. Foreign rhetoric regarding the CIA is seen as exaggerated or even paranoid, at least hypersensitive, and possibly phony, certainly not the reaction of rational, logical people. The U.S. thus names an ex-director of the CIA as ambassador to Iran and then is surprised that the Embassy is perceived as a "den of spies." It is not hard to understand why the election of another former director of the CIA as Vice-President might affect foreign perceptions of the U.S. and its policies.

Pursuing image analysis goes far toward making differing views of history understandable. A useful exercise is comparing history texts used in schools. To get a contrasting sense of national self-image, one might well compare the eighth grade history text used in their country of assignment with the one they used as a student.

MINDSETS AND NATIONAL SECURITY

While most people working internationally are not directly involved in national security affairs or international conflict resolution, mindsets related to this most fundamental aspect of conducting international relations deserves special attention.

The problem is, what can we say here that has not already been said many times? The literature on this subject—which we will not try to summarize—is extensive and the role of misperception has been a frequent theme. Psychological warfare is a subject in itself. One book that sets the agenda for this kind of analysis bears the interesting title *Psychology and the Prevention of Nuclear War* (Ralph K. White, ed.).[9]

Our main purpose here is simply to demonstrate the need for more critical analysis of the mindset factor in highly important security affairs. To do this we will rather arbitrarily select two areas for brief discussion that illustrate the far-reaching consequences mindsets have in the way we think about national defense and related matters. One is the especially American predisposition to calculate military strength rather narrowly in quantitative terms, that is, in terms of numbers and cost, rather than in terms of such ultimately decisive factors as national cohesion and will. The second is the matter of calculating the psychological cement that holds alliances together in times of stress—a fundamental in any security equation.

Calculation of military and defense capabilities. We often find a process of selective perception and reasoning at work when policy makers, the Congress, and the public debate national security issues. It is remarkable that despite evidence to the contrary from previous conflicts, attention to American defense policy seems to be fixed on the idea that the quantity and sophistication of military hardware is a true index of national security. There is even a tendency to equate the size of a defense budget with actual military effectiveness as if there were a linear relationship between dollars spent and combat performance. This view is applied to the capability of other nations as well. Vast effort is expended in intelligence collection and analysis to compute the exact balance in missiles, warheads, tanks, aircraft and technical performance.

The myopia involved in this calculation is breathtaking. It would appear that the ability of a nation to prevail is based on the equipment it possesses, as if the equipment did the fighting all by itself. Admittedly, this is an oversimplification; national security professionals do recognize the importance of human skills, organization, and morale. Yet, Americans have a habit of conceptualizing problems in mechanistic and quantitative terms, so it is easier for the public and its leaders to think in such terms and debate and plan accordingly.

Unhappily, the crucial human factors are not easily quantified, even though military outcomes are greatly affected by them. National cohesion, trust in leadership, self-confidence, sense of purpose, initiative, adeptness, etc., determine how equipment will in fact be used. By all the quantitative calculations we made, the North Vietnamese could not win; they could not even hold out much longer. But they did, because the calculations did not take into account the human "intangibles" on both sides.

The Shah of Iran, to cite another example, was extraordinarily well equipped, but that equipment neither kept him in power nor proved very effective in defeating the Iraqis after it was inherited by the Khomeini regime. French self-assurance in calculating their hardware did not go far in the Maginot line. There is a tendency to rationalize the success of insurgent forces by claiming they have access to extraordinary materiel resources even when they do not exist or do not reach the proportions imagined. The famous Ho Chi Minh trail supply route "explained" the success of the Viet Cong; equipment supplied from Cuba via Nicaragua was the fallback explanation for El Salvadoran rebel strength. Clearly, some method for judging military capability less subject to misplaced emphasis is needed.

More attention has to be directed toward such questions as *why* people fight—or coalesce behind leaders or side with insurgents—in the first place. In estimating the performance of military organizations, one has to factor in how the people involved think about command, responsibility, strategy, even the value of life itself. Also, supplying, deploying, and maintaining complicated machinery is a function of appropriate culturally-based ways of thinking. This was a highly significant facet of Israeli military success in planning and executing the raid at Entebbe, involving the rescue of passengers held hostage after an airline hijacking.

Sometimes the gap in thinking about military operations is considerable. A U.S. Navy officer recalled his frustration in getting his South Vietnamese counterparts to use river patrol boats for their intended strategic purpose and not for operating a moonlight ferryboat service or for excursions for relatives.

Pursuit of security through alliances. It is simply fundamental that no nation in the late twentieth century will achieve any substantial degree of security by going it alone. Security means alliances of some kind. As alliances are matters of perceived common interest, common advantage, threat, identity, moral purpose, etc., they are ultimately based on and held together by psychological factors, by mindsets. While we think of alliances as formally negotiated in rational, calculated self-interest, the *will* to form alliances and a people's readiness to support them is the foundation of their strength and durability.

If an alliance is based on single issues or short-range objectives, its strength and duration will depend on the strength and duration of the issue. If an alliance is based only on mutual fear or a sense of having a common foe, it will be viable only so long as those purposes last. The same is true of alliances directed toward temporary goals, such as the Southeast Asia Treaty Organization (SEATO). As circumstances have changed, the parties to SEATO have questioned its usefulness. New Zealand, for example, has concluded that nuclear-armed U.S. vessels in New Zealand ports are more of a threat than a protection and has refused cooperation. On the other hand, NATO rests on somewhat more of an enduring sense of common purpose among at least some of its members, the United States and Great Britain, especially. But this more enduring common view is not shared by all its members, so that the pact loses cohesiveness at the edges.

Fundamentally, judging the politics of alliances requires a study of the underlying values involved and careful examination of the degree to which those values are broadly shared. The excesses of the Nazi era evoked outside Germany a widely shared sense of violated values, and hence a firm base for a broad alliance and determined cooperation and sacrifice. Other cases—the imposition of martial law in Poland in 1982, for instance, or OPEC's manipulation of oil prices—provided a somewhat shakier base for cohesion and common effort. Even in the face of terrorism, a moral common ground for taking concerted action formed only slowly and competed with other separate interests and perceptions of the threat. When in 1986 the Reagan administration was caught dealing in arms with Iran while simultaneously urging its NATO allies not to, the sense of mutual confidence suffered a severe blow.

THE MANY EFFECTS OF NEWS FLOW

A discussion of perception and reasoning in international political affairs is not complete without restressing the significance of news flow. As an all-pervading data and information base, news is a fundamental variable in the way the international relations process works. *News flow becomes the central nervous system for global political relations.* It is the gatekeeper determining what the central issues will be. It sets the agenda to a large degree and often defines the issues for both the public and decision makers. In addition to what has been said in earlier chapters, several facets of news processing deserve highlighting here in the context of making judgments about mindsets in political and governmental matters.

First, what people—including decision makers—know and understand about issues and events is often a function of the way news is gathered and processed. News reporters and editors are themselves de facto international political analysts; their judgmental skills are just as important a part of the international relations process as that of diplomats and intelligence experts. Like other people, they are information processing machines, and their perception and interpretation are subject to the same psychological processes as anyone else's. The lens through which they see the world is culture-tinted; they project implicit assumptions onto events; they draw on limited sources of information. In short, they inject into everybody's key information base all the mindset considerations we have been talking about.

News and media services, then, supply a major part of the cognitive base for interpreting international events by selecting what is to be news and by deciding the way events are conceptualized. If an event does not pass a newsworthiness threshold in the minds of news processors, it is not likely to reach and be taken into account by the public and possibly not considered in the specialist's calculations either, at least not with the same urgency. When news is reported, its effect will already be pre-programmed to some degree by the words selected to report it, or by the way a television shot is angled or background is included or panned out. Does the news report refer to dissidents or the opposition? Foreign sympathizers or interventionists? Does the television viewer see a leader at a state banquet or visiting a housing project for workers?

Managing the news has itself become an international issue, especially as the Third World sees itself on the dependency end of an international news flow that is owned and operated by the richer nations that have become overpowering information societies. This has given rise to a debate on the need for a "New World Information Order," especially in UNESCO. All the questions raised in the section above on self-image are considerations in the debate, with the addition of a sense of being the pawn or victim of an established technology and news dissemination system. For the international community, what is news and who decides? How is national sovereignty affected as news flows across boundaries? When does one country's news become another country's entertainment? What is the effect when news becomes simply a commercial product and is selected to sell as such? Conflicting views of these matters abound.

At the heart of this debate are widely differing conceptions of the social purpose of the news. In the West free news flow has served the "fourth estate" function, providing some of the checks and balances by which a democratic government operates. News is meant to inform the public. It also functions as a business enterprise, serving as a source of profit; those who supply the news compete in a free marketplace. By this system, so its proponents argue, the news function is kept free of government control. In other societies, government monopoly in news dissemination is seen as a proper and necessary means not so much of informing but of *educating* the people and of managing public attitudes. News thus serves a different social purpose. This has been the outlook of the Castro government in Cuba. If the news transmission resources are limited, social objectives may demand that priorities be established for media and news services; using them to promote development or social harmony may be the overriding consideration.[10]

Further, news operations have become not simply the external messenger reporting the international relations process, but a part of events themselves. News is often an instrument of policy execution, to wit, the news leak, managed news, timed releases, and the use of news as international propaganda. It also becomes part of the denouement of international relations when, for instance, dissident or insurgent groups promote their causes by creating a media event or use the international media to bypass governments in reaching public audiences. Sometimes news coverage either *is* the event or creates the event. Former Egyptian President Anwar Sadat's impasse-breaking visit to Israel was precipitated by the intervention of American television reporters who started the ball rolling by asking Sadat, in effect, why he did not go to Israel personally and break the stand-off in relations. When he said that he had not been invited, the reporters proceeded to ask Israel's Prime Minister Begin why not. The invitation and the visit which followed were a genuine media happening with far-reaching consequences.

We should note that international news coverage and reporting requires a skill basically different from that needed for domestic reporting. In the case of news flow *within* a society, the *context* of news is largely known by the reader or viewer. Hence, the meaning of news can be transmitted with some degree of accuracy by objectively reporting the event. But in international news coverage and reporting, the context and meaning have to be transmitted in addition, along with the description of the event itself, if news is to accurately inform. This is a vastly more difficult task for all the reasons elaborated in this book and is only beginning to be appreciated in selecting and training international journalists.

In any case, it is apparent that one of the crucial items on the future international agenda will be to decide how to make institutions which manage the news flow into a reliable central nervous system for an interdependent world in which problems increasingly will have to be resolved at an international level. To the degree that news contributes to misperception or fails to supply a dependable data base for understanding international issues and events, it will be part of the problem in international political affairs rather than a resource for problem or conflict resolution.

Contrasting Mindsets in Development and Technical Assistance Affairs

While to the public international relations may seem to consist primarily of such major issues as East-West relations, nuclear confrontation, NATO relationships, or international trade, large numbers of practitioners of international relations spend most of their time on something much less publicized, the planning and implementation of Third World development. Loans for development projects are negotiated by governments or by international organizations and private financial institutions. Universities contract to supply technical assistance teams. Third World governments decide on candidates for advanced overseas training. Industries plan and establish manufacturing plants in the developing world; engineering companies design dams and power plants. Religious groups, private foundations, government agencies, and the Peace Corps take on community development projects. Suppliers fill orders for medicines, machine tools, spare parts, and communication equipment. Mangers on both sides of the development gap try to orchestrate it all against defined development goals and basic ideas of how to reach them. And all of this is accompanied by a great deal of international dialogue and negotiation, which takes place at project sites, in conference rooms, or, indeed, in newspaper editorials and political pronouncements.

International development assistance is thus clearly an area in which mindset analysis should receive a high priority.

The glaring contrasts in the degree of economic and political development and in the accompanying value systems and mindsets give rise to widely differing views of development issues—of priorities, strategies, goals, even of the probability for success. The simple fact of having been brought up in a modern, industrialized, achievement-oriented society rather than a traditional and less developed one programs people to perceive the many aspects of the development process differently. Deeper cultural contrasts lead to still more profound mismatches in implicit assumptions and conventional wisdom.

The literature on development is vast, of course, so our contribution here will be confined to applying the cross-cultural and comparative perception approach to several salient problem areas.

DEVELOPMENT MANAGERS —THE VIEW FROM INSIDE A DEVELOPING SOCIETY

Much of what is written on the strategy of development is, like this book, produced by people whose point of view is from the outside looking in, that is, from the perspective of specialists from the developed world who diagnose and prescribe for a client whose real life experience they have not shared. Their colleagues in the Third World, development managers and others, can enter intellectually into discussions based on these perspectives because they reflect the assumptions and logic of an international development fraternity. Indeed, a kind of international subculture exists to enhance interaction for all those engaged in development. They can all talk of investment rates, infrastructures, human resources development, and even speak in the tongues of acronyms that designate the many agencies and programs through which development is promoted—USAID, UNDP., etc.

But when it comes to implementing plans, with real development projects carried out by real people working through real local institutions, then development planners on the inside must view the project from their own cultural and national vantage point. The basis for dialogue changes as the differing perspectives of developed and developing societies become more germane—as development schemes move from theory to implementation. What are some of the probable operative components of Third World development specialists' outlook?

In the first place, since they are themselves part of the local social and political system, they will have internalized a native's understanding of how that system works. They will, for example, have absorbed the inner logic of the way the upper classes deal with the peasantry or the way people contend for and use personal loyalties and political power. They will share a certain feeling of resignation to the inertia that goes with traditional society and its values. They will be influenced by religious precepts affecting the way the very ideas of modernization and progress are viewed, whether they still consciously adhere to those precepts or not.

Those who are inside a culture have a sixth sense for the customary—and even the devious and supposedly unsanctioned—ways by which individuals and groups contend for advantage. They know how group cleavages hidden to the outsider can preclude cooperation or collective effort. In short, they have an inner sense of all the reasons why a system is *not* likely to change to the designs of planners, or at least not change rapidly, and why conflicting expectations and priorities may affect local perception of new proposals or innovations. For example, when land reform is proposed, even though they have consciously discarded the fetters of traditionalism, they may still hold subtle, semiconscious expectations regarding the social relationships that go with an authoritarian and hierarchical culture and sense in part of their minds an aura of nonreality in the outsider's vision of a new system of small landholdings or cooperatives, or the expectation that former landowners will beat a graceful retreat.

Then one must consider the images insiders have of themselves as agents of change. Here again development managers from the nonindustrialized world will define their roles in ways that in all probability will contrast sharply with the self-images held by their working counterparts from industrialized countries. The Third World managers come, after all, from societies where the change agent's role and social prestige will probably be quite ill defined. They might even be considered marginal or, at best, mavericks working on the cutting edge of their society. Certainly their status will not be well institutionalized; even the middle-class groups to which they will most likely belong may be more ad hoc than established Western middle classes. Their societies will not reenforce them in their calling. They will sense the inertia of the ever-present poor and the barriers created by provincial suspicions. And they will feel strains—not shared by their outside advisors—following from the special challenges put to their capabilities, resources and steadfastness of purpose. Their job security might be uncertain. They will have their own personal weaknesses and appetites for enjoying the fruits of modernization. Using one's position for personal advantage is simply common sense in many, if not most cultures. Thus, their personal agendas and the development agenda might not always be compatible. Development managers from the Third World need a different kind of idealism from that of their developed world opposites. *The view from the inside looking out is quite different from the view outside looking in.*

In the end Third World development planners, in responding to the necessity of bridging cultures, have to develop multicultural personalities themselves and be ready to switch from one to another as the occasion demands and somehow continue to be sure of who they are and what they are doing in the process. This is an extraordinary task in personal cognitive organization. It is the more difficult because they not only have to handle the personal stress that goes with playing contradictory roles in differing sociocultural arenas, but they also have to maintain their vision and an intellectual command of the meaning and social purpose of the change process over which they preside. Leaders who have risen to these demands are among the towering personalities of this century. Whatever their success or even degree of political attractiveness outside their societies, people like Mahatma Gandhi (India), Julius Nyerere (Tanzania), Anwar Sadat (Egypt), Mao Zedong (China), and Lee Kuan Yew (Singapore), to name a few, illustrate the complexity of mind that can be produced at the interface of cultures and amid the processes of change.

ATTRIBUTING CAUSE FOR UNDERDEVELOPMENT

One's mindset regarding the *reasons why* a given country is behind in national development would obviously affect perception and reasoning about the issues and problems arising in international development relations.

From the perspective of an outsider from a developed nation, the explanation for underdevelopment may naively focus on the ways in which *they are not like us.* In this mode of thought, stereotyping comes easily into play. The idea of racial inferiority seems plausible and is an attitude still found among ethnocentric Western observers who are not really convinced that development efforts can succeed in some countries beyond limited levels of sophistication. In such cases the lack of competencies and skills needed for development is emphasized; basic education and training is prescribed, usually accompanied by a patronizing attitude and a skepticism that it will accomplish much.

At a more analytical level, the diagnosis of observers from the industrialized world turns to economic and social systems and to factors and prerequisites for development as seen from the developed world's perspective: management experience, industrial infrastructure, energy resources, rates of savings and investments, the state of financial and commercial institutions, the terms of international trade and balance of payments ratios, and so forth. And most important, advisors from the industrialized world *see themselves and their own country as part of the solution, never part of the problem.* They represent progress, they want to provide assistance; their zeal often verges on that of the missionary. They look to the future and tend to downgrade the past. And they are not likely to see their own success as having been achieved at the expense of people now seeking to share the benefits of modern development.

But from the developing world's view, it is more probable that the *success of the industrial nations will in fact be seen as part of the problem.* It is not hard to understand how their past experiences with today's economically powerful countries might lead to differences in identifying the cause of underdevelopment. Typically, lesser developed societies have been on the receiving end of some kind of colonial rule and today are "have-not" countries. From a post-colonial, have-not perspective, it is reasonable to assume that the well-being of developed nations bas been gained at the expense of one's own underdevelopment. Imperialism, exploitation of raw materials and cheap labor, the power and wealth of multinational corporations, and the sheer unfair advantage which governments and economic institutions of industrialized countries appear to have in the marketplace all seem to be designed to perpetuate underdevelopment, not to pose solutions for Third World difficulties. It is thus easy to attribute intention: *It is the industrialized world's objective in its own self-interest to keep the Third World in a subservient position.* Here we have a full-blown mindset which becomes more pronounced where it is reinforced by a Marxist interpretation of history—a cognitive framework which tends to direct perceptions toward just that kind of manipulative cause and effect relationship.

If one sees development in one country as being the cause of underdevelopment in another, the remedy is readily suggested: a new, more equitable distribution of advantage. Hence the calls for a New World Economic Order, and the intellectual debates and international conferences that have followed. The probability of agreement is slim, however, since the two sides will not, in effect, be talking about the same problem. Basic assumptions, practical diagnoses and intuitive feelings about what can actually be done differ too much.

A predisposition to put the blame on developed countries for impeding development elsewhere produces certain spin-offs that affect international development relations. For example, it gives rise to a preference for multilateral assistance programs, like those extended through the World Bank, over bilateral programs involving direct agreements between the United States and a given developing country. This is especially true if the terms of assistance require compliance with such conditions as enacting new tax measures, buying equipment from the donor country, conforming with technical specifications, engaging foreign technicians or contractors or agreeing to loans being disbursed on a step-by-step basis as work is completed and inspected.

If the recipient of the loan suspects that the more powerful country was the *cause* of the problem in the first place, this "big brother" approach grates on national sensitivities. Hence, what starts out as "development assistance" becomes political confrontation. The conditions imposed become intolerable interventions into the internal affairs of the recipient country. If money is borrowed and is to be paid back, then it is felt that the funds should be subject to the borrower's decision making and management. Consequently, in many bilateral projects, assistance is far from politically neutral. When assistance also carries, or appears to carry, political strings, such as votes in the U.N., access to military bases, or opposition to specific ideological movements, the barriers to reaching agreement on "development assistance" can be considerable.

I recall a case in which U.S. officials were considering a loan for a small program in a Latin American country. The loan would in effect simply help the government maintain its cash flow to pay public servants, such as school teachers, police, and office workers, through a transition period between the rule of a fallen military junta and the election of a new, more democratic government. The loan objective was purely political; without it an already unstable situation would be exacerbated and prospects for a new constitutional government would be more uncertain. But the loan would produce no development. In fact, it would only add to an already heavy debt-servicing load.

Therefore, U.S. assistance officials decided to get as much development mileage from it as possible. The loan, they said, would be made on the condition that certain tax reform measures be enacted and certain fiscal procedures be remodeled along more efficient lines. The officials of the recipient government objected. They argued that by the very nature of their interim mandate as a caretaker government, they could not make commitments for the new government that would come to power after the elections. So they resisted. The Americans twisted arms, believing the money was needed so badly that their conditions would have to be accepted. Honor then became an additional consideration on the recipient's side. But there was also an element of urgency; the U.S. budget authorization under which the loan would be made was to expire soon, at the end of the fiscal year. Finally, the interim president gave in and pressured his minister of finance to sign the agreement. He did, under protest, at 10:00 p.m. on the last day, only two hours before the clock ran out. He resigned the following morning. For whatever it is worth, the interim government did survive to usher in a new constitutional government; the tax reforms survived, but only technically, and the sense of trust among all concerned fell another notch.

Other things being equal, then, the political and emotional preference among lesser developed countries is for multilateral assistance rather than bilateral agreements with single countries. While multinational lenders also impose conditions, they seem, from the perspective of the recipient country, more neutral, the loan more a matter of technical merit and objective regulation than exploitation, interference, or patronizing "big brotherism." Even though the politicking behind the scenes in setting conditions or making concessions is intense in the World Bank and other international lending institutions, the multilateral umbrella tends to defuse the threat to sovereignty and to pride.

A predisposition to suspect motives also tends to cloud programs which donor nations see as entirely altruistic, such as disaster relief, Peace Corps projects, or the charity and service projects of religious groups. The difficulty is that the donors usually have little experience being on the receiving end of such relationships, and especially little basis for empathizing with those who are *always* the receivers. The question is: What is the psychological reaction when local leaders time and again have to depend on foreign assistance for emergency grain, as in the U.S. PL 480 program, or on medical teams when floods and earthquakes strike? (How is one to react when developed countries send their "children"—as some perceived early Peace Corps volunteers—to lend technical advice?)

Donors anticipate appreciation and gratitude for their efforts, or at the least friendship or perhaps reciprocal favors as circumstances allow. When this response is not forthcoming, or the help is resisted in the first place, congressmen protest the ungratefulness, and relief organizations and church groups feel frustrated. Communication falls on hard times.

India provides a salient example, with its long history of receiving humanitarian aid during times of starvation or disaster. When independence was gained, many Americans expected in India a warm ally on the democratic front. Instead, India turned rapidly to neutrality, vocally disapproving of American international behavior and even lecturing the U.S. on the shortcomings of its democratic practices at home. Occasionally, in seeming violation of their own best interest, India went out of its way to *avoid* assistance. During one period of food shortage, instead of accepting still more American aid in what was seen as a demeaning relationship, they purchased wheat from the Soviet Union at a higher price. This in turn led the Soviet Union to buy more wheat from the U.S. to make up the difference, and bread prices went up for American families! Such is the impact of mindset factors in an era of interdependence.

THE CULTURE AND PERSONALITY FACTOR IN DEVELOPMENT

Several years ago a *Wall Street Journal* reporter's attention was attracted to a Venezuelan plan to drastically alter that country's approach to education. The plan called for a new cabinet post of "Minister of State for the Development of Human Intelligence." The incumbent of that post proposed to increase Venezuelan competence in the modern world by teaching thinking skills. He argued that the mathematics taught at Harvard and in Moscow were the same as that taught in Caracas and Bogota and that the potential of the students was the same. But the results were different. Why? He suggested that by some means students in developed countries were taught to think. In Venezuela, on the other hand, they were taught to memorize and repeat without any creative or analytical effort. Thus, a "learn to think" project was being introduced in a number of educational programs from primary schools to the armed forces. The early results seemed promising, though some critics of the plan worried that success might compound Venezuela's problems: the political system could not survive 16 million "thinking" citizens![1]

I also recall from graduate field work days an extensive community development project in the lower valley of the Santiago River in the state of Nayarit in Mexico. The director of the project, Professor Mario Aguilera Dorantes came into the valley armed with substantial new resources for education. The public assumed that first priority would go to the needed expansion of the high school in the central town and to making sure that all the villages had primary schools. To their surprise, highest priority went to establishing *kindergartens* in every village. The director explained that what he wanted to get across had to be learned before the first grade—children had to learn to think of themselves as creative agents, had to learn patterns of cooperation and to learn how to learn. In short the director sought to develop new basic personality traits that would sustain the other innovations he wished to introduce in the valley. He wanted to create a new kind of people in the area, and at the kindergarten level it was already very late to mold personality structure.

In Chapter III we stressed that the way people perceive their environment, the forces within it, and their relation to it, is a function of the way that culture programs their internal computers. Hence, patterns of personality vary around the world. When this notion is applied to national social and economic development, we are asking in effect whether some basic personality patterns are more adapted to living in modern industrial and political systems than others, and whether some are more adaptable to change itself than others. If this is so, the logic follows that if a society is to "develop," changes must be made, not simply in the kinds of knowledge and skills acquired, but in patterns of personality, in fundamental values and habits of reasoning, and in the most basic interpretation of the conditions of living and people's response to them. Lawrence Harrison makes much the same proposition in his book *Underdevelopment Is a State of Mind.*[2]

If this thesis is true, then the current heavy emphasis on manipulating quantifiable economic factors falls short of what is needed. Efforts to transplant practices, techniques and institutions in psycho-cultural soil that does not contain the cognitive prerequisites for them face an uphill battle. This would be true whether the development design were democratic, autocratic, socialistic, or communistic. The Communists recognize this, of course. Hence their overbearing emphasis on controlling formative education and disrupting the patterns of family and social relationships, all to assure rapid and consistent change. This approach was particularly evident in China where the family has been such a vital part of the traditional socialization process, though, in the entrepreneurial new China, one wonders how deep an impact the Mao regime actually had.

It has long been recognized that if it were possible simply to transplant a culture group with mindsets already oriented to economic development into an underdeveloped region, the course of development there would differ even if all other factors remained the same. One of the long remembered stories from the early days of Philippine independence involves a visit by the late Senator Allen J. Ellender soon after World War II and the end of Japanese occupation of the islands. Resentments against the Japanese still raged fiercely. The senator, however, had just visited Japan and had been greatly impressed by Japanese efforts in their own reconstruction. When he arrived in Manila, the local press was on hand at the airport for any newsworthy statements. They were not disappointed. What the Philippines should do to enhance their economic development, said the Senator, was to open their country to Japanese immigration. Copies of the outraged news reports were collectors' items for many years.

Yet, despite the senator's gaffe, differing populations can be expected to perceive the potential for their environment in different ways, according to their cultural backgrounds. The Israelis have viewed the possibilities of their desert environment in ways very different from those of other societies that have occupied the same area for generations. The Japanese manage their economic activities differently from the Filipinos, and Filipinos manage theirs differently from Indonesians. There are instances in which attempts have been made to attract populations whose cultural characteristics were such that it was believed they would enhance development of some kind. Italian immigration was sought by Venezuela at one time; Japanese and Okinawans have been encouraged to migrate to Brazil, Mennonites to Paraguay, and Germans and Scandinavians to the United Stated. The unique economic role played by colonies of overseas Chinese cannot be overlooked. Even in military affairs there are ethnic preferences in selecting mercenaries because of attitudes toward armed combat and military discipline.

It is useful to look deeper for an explanation of why this selective transplanting seems to work. In part the answer is found in observable cultural practices, such as institutionalized ways of doing things, knowledge and learned skills, readiness to use modern tools, and advanced and efficient production processes. But the deeper levels of culture, where cognitive preparation has conditioned a given group to think and conceptualize activity as it does, have not been frequently explored in development strategy analysis. These factors are relatively intangible and hard to quantify. And they cannot be easily manipulated by simply changing the technical conditions for development and change.

Therefore, consistent with our purposes in building our mindset and comparative perception approach, let us single out for analytical emphasis in this discussion the thinking and reasoning base for development which is supplied by culture. Our proposition, as has been stated, is that whether taken into account by planners or not, economic and social change means a change in "deep culture," in such fundamentals as values, implicit assumptions, and patterns of reasoning, that is, in the built-in cultural predispositions by which people view economic and related institutional activities. When this is taken into account, one's understanding of development and change processes is much enlarged.

What are some of the specific areas in which mindsets appear to be most significant? Certainly one is management, where abstract thinking about cause and effect, coordinating activities, anticipating contingencies, and fitting new projects into an overall institutional system is clearly required. Third World developers find that while many of the fundamental skills needed for development have been learned by their societies, managing them effectively is much more challenging. Management competence is more elusive than "technical skill." It is proving much more difficult to transfer management practices across cultures because they constitute more than "skills." They are, or at least are imbedded in, a way of thinking.

In many cases, especially in countries which have emerged from colonial administration since World War II, expatriates have been retained to provide managerial assistance. For example, in the Ivory Coast, French administrators have been kept on for this purpose. In Zambia, to use another African example, the goal has been to replace expatriate managers with Zambian nationals in development organizing and planning. For Zambia, therefore, management *training* is a priority concern. Whether it is managing a business or a parastatal corporation, administering a bureaucracy, or organizing a national development plan, the talent required is of a different order than the technical know-how to rotate crops, teach mechanical engineering, keep accounts, or treat disease.

Thus, value orientations and mindsets become essential variables. This is true for all social sectors, from workers and farmers to mid-level technical and commercial managers to executives. A few of the more significant cognitive factors that affect economic and social behavior can be singled out for attention.

Orientation toward the self. One particularly relevant concern for development is how individuals differ in the degree to which they think of *themselves* as active change agents with the ability to produce effects in the world around them, an aspect of cause and effect reasoning. In culture and personality studies this is often stated as a contrast between *fatalism* on the one hand and an *activist/optimist* orientation on the other.

In the fatalistic mold one is socialized to think of the environment as being an arena in which one must deal with forces over which one has little or no control. Life and its circumstances are given. The individual's task is to adjust to them rather than manipulate them. If one is to effect change, it is more logical to appeal to the larger forces that are seen to be the controlling agents—the divine, the government, perhaps stronger and more influential people. Speculation as to what fate has in store becomes a popular theme in legend and literature, and "luck" and the lottery are taken very seriously. Obviously, this mindset is not conducive to operating in a modern scientific and industrialized world. It is, nonetheless, a common feature of traditional societies.

The activist mindset conceives of the universe and its forces as a complex set of causes and effects and as an arena in which the individual can intervene as an actor to exercise some degree of control over events. The individual not only *can* exercise this control, in some cases the value system makes intervention an imperative and even elevates work as such to a prime value. We have noted that in the case of American society, we find an all-pervading emphasis on the value of achievement and the rewards that go with it. Americans are optimistic and believe in progress and in the happy endings that result from human effort and perseverance. It is a problem-solving, activistic society and as such has tended to become a model for modernization and development.[3]

Achievement motivation. As has been mentioned earlier, achievement motivation is another important factor in powering development, at least in the Western world. Americans, it is argued, absorb in their upbringing a particular psychological need to achieve, which translates into characteristically American forms of entrepreneurship. Studies have found that this need is not present to the same degree in all cultures. Obviously, then, in cases where reliance is placed on American prescriptions for development, the presence or absence of an American-style achievement motivation could be quite significant. What role can entrepreneurship play in a developing society if this psychological framework is missing? Could it be introduced in less time than the several generations which are normally required for substantial value changes? David McCelland's experiments in India to do just that ended with mixed results.[4]

Time. A third area in which cultures exhibit great variation in cognitive preparation for modernization is in the conceptualization of time, including time sequence, use of time, and most especially, the conception of the future—to which the idea of progress so directly relates. Societies vary greatly in this regard. Continuity with the past and tradition is a central theme in many societies. The Arabic language, for instance, provides only tenuous linguistic structures for talking about the future, which, by religious precept, is not man's concern but that of the Divine. Some languages and cultures are very present-oriented. I would argue that this is a feature of Philippine society which in many ways makes it a very pleasant milieu for enjoying such pleasures and associations as are available at the moment, but not one to sustain the development planner. At another extreme is traditional Buddhist culture, which treats time and one's personal involvement with it as evolving cycles rather than as a linear progression. This is so foreign to Western thinking that Western development planners tend simply to reject any implications it might have for economic development.

Tomas R. Fillol, in discussing economic development in Argentina, argues that the particular orientation to time there is part of a basic sense of impotence in controlling the forces of nature. He suggests that in believing in luck and the destiny of the nation, the Argentine "does not *live or work* for the future; *he contemplates its image...*"[5]

Time orientation can affect the ease with which people fall into step with the modernizing process. Will one save capital for an uncertain tomorrow, rather than enjoy it in a known today? Will one plan with conviction, sacrifice against future goals, and actually believe that a series of purposive actions leads to a desired end?

Social relationships. In moving toward the more complex and industrialized life that goes with development, a national character has to evolve that is consistent with new kinds of social relations, where one deals more often with strangers or with people to whom one relates only in specific work or institutional contexts. This calls for new conceptions of personal relationships and new values to go with them. By what internalized logic will people cooperate with fellow citizens or identify with partial strangers to accomplish a common purpose? By what faith will people extend confidence to impersonal government agencies, commercial and financial institutions, or even to a neighborhood credit cooperative? Within this expanded social environment, people also have to play a greater variety of roles; hence, a developing society must supply new definitions of role behavior.

If development is to take place in a democratic format, this process of creating a new psychological base for social relations is especially difficult to manage because needed changes in attitude and belief are left to the volition of the individual or are presented through education that tries—democratically—to persuade rather than coerce. New forms of social behavior are thus generated slowly. In the case of authoritarian governments, and the Communists stand out as a prime example, coercion might in the short run change behavior, even without changes in the mindset of the masses. But in the long run, the goal is to change underlying beliefs and idea patterns. The application of this strategy in the Soviet Union, China and Cuba is well known. Other authoritarian governments have tried variations on it; the case of Attaturk in Turkey is classic, as is that of the Shah of Iran. Both found difficulty in bucking established cultural patterns and building a popular support base for modernization, the consequences of which were demonstrated spectacularly by the takeover of Iran by fundamentalist ayatollahs.

Tanzania and Zambia present other examples of attempts to address the belief and attitude base in an effort to sustain development. In Tanzania, Julius Nyerere's *Ujamaa* program was based on traditional concepts of cooperation and sharing. In Zambia, with its many languages and identities, the perceived need has been to engender a sense of national cohesion in order to lay the foundation for collective national effort. During one period every station break on radio and television carried the slogan, "One Zambia, one people."

Returning again to Fillol's study of development in Argentina and his analysis of Argentine national character (cited above), he notes that some cultural traits constitute a barrier to development because they hinder the emergence of social relationships that "enable individuals to act concertedly in the pursuit of common goals and interests."[6] For example, with the valued person in the executive position being the one who *is* somebody, rather than one who *does* something, one may find people with authority more inclined to accumulate and hold that authority rather than delegate it. Relationships between superiors and subordinates that go with this kind of value orientation will also probably inhibit initiative. And we might expect that the rules for advancement that would fit the demands of modern industrial relations would not be easily accommodated. These value orientations are related to those of the "public man" concept discussed earlier.

All this places a different light on national social and economic development. Conventional modern economic and institutional analytical approaches do not go far enough. One needs to calculate how culturally determined mindsets can be changed to enhance the development process, or, on the other hand, how development strategies can be adapted to existing belief and value patterns. It is fundamental social science that new mindsets cannot be taught easily or simply passed on from the developed world as readily as technical knowledge or skills might be.

Abstract thinking and reasoning. At the very least, living as an active participant in a "developed" society calls for the ability to engage in abstract thinking and reasoning. As work becomes more specialized and interrelated with the work of others, and as associations with a wider range of individuals make social life more complex, "reality" is more to be perceived in the abstract, more to be pieced together in mental processes.

This issue of being able to think in the abstract is illustrated nicely in Richard McKenna's novel, *The Sand Pebbles*[7]. In it the central character, Holman, presides over the steam engines of an aging U.S. Navy gunboat, "San Pablo," in the Yangtze River basin in China in the 1920s. One of his pet projects is teaching a coolie helper, Po-han, the theory of steam energy by which pressure mounts in pipes, pistons move, and water re-forms in return systems. It is one thing for Po-han to imitate Holman's routine in operating the engine, another to reason about what is going on *unseen* inside the system and to control the process. Eventually, Holman delights in Po-han's ability to move to a level of abstract comprehension and to work with machinery in a totally new way.

Abstracting is called for continuously in the daily routines of modern social and economic systems, from budgeting and setting production levels to engaging in hypothetical reasoning in science. Cultures differ greatly in the degree to which people are programmed to engage in abstract reasoning, and when such reasoning is fundamental to the success of a given development effort, limiting the program to superficial transfers of technology and skills does not fit the bill.

DILEMMAS IN DEVELOPMENT IMPLEMENTATION

We noted above that the personal psychological orientation for directing development programs is quite different for the person operating from inside the recipient culture than for the one on the outside who is providing resources and prescribing their use. Here we will enlarge on that theme by posing several dilemmas relating to development strategy that illustrate some of the differing perspectives brought to the implementation process. These are dilemmas that typically emerge from the mindsets of Third World developers and from the situations in which they find themselves in the actual routine of carrying out projects.

What part of the society should get first priority for development? If "development" is interpreted to mean primarily a matter of higher standards of living, will limited resources be directed toward those living in poverty—to the "poorest of the poor," to use recent U.S. development jargon—or toward the developing middle sectors where some success can more realistically be expected and where many local development practitioners themselves have vested interests? Or even toward existing business or other professional elites with justification based on some kind of "trickle down" theory? It can be argued—or rationalized—that sustained development depends on the existence of a viable middle class made up of people with education, technical know-how, and adequate facilities, and that such people need a salary and living conditions attractive enough to prevent them from emigrating to more attractive opportunities abroad. Might not the middle class be the logical starting point in long-range planning? Perhaps reaching the "poorest of the poor" is, in practical application, a socio-economic nonstarter, a concept which is more appealing to the ideals and consciences of advisors from the industrialized countries than it is responsive to either local social and economic realities or to the outlooks of the people who must execute development plans.

What kinds of projects are most satisfying? Those inside an economically less developed country look at project proposals against a background of frustration with their circumstances and with a keen appetite to feel themselves part of the modern world—and soon. Hence, the project that produces a tangible result quickly or provides visible symbols of modernity tends to evoke greater enthusiasm than the ten-year irrigation plan or the project to combat intestinal diseases in remote rural villages. Especially if resources appear limited and the prospects for broad development seem remote, the temptation is great to give priority to projects which may not necessarily contribute as directly as others to long-range productivity, but which will make life better in urban centers and enhance the national image by providing the symbols of twentieth-century existence. Consequently, interest is focused more easily on urban housing and water systems, telephone networks, modern hospitals and clinics, sports stadiums, airlines that carry the flag on international routes, prestigious conference centers, university buildings and even parks and monuments.

Will planners give priority to development economics or welfare economics? This dilemma is not simply a matter of which socio-economic class to favor, but a question related to a more profound political fact of life. If some public demands, and particularly mass urban demands, are not met quickly, the stability essential for any planning may be cut short. Social services, welfare programs, jobs, cheap transportation, affordable basic foodstuffs cannot be delayed until overall national development takes hold. Yet, resources spent of food subsidies and lowcost housing translate only indirectly into higher productivity and may delay establishing the infrastructure essential to industrial expansion or transporting agricultural products to market or export commodities to ports. When making choices, it is well to remember that street demonstrations command immediate attention, while long-range needs for systematic economic restructuring are more abstract. If the tenure of a political administration is uncertain at best and the jobs of those who must implement development accordingly unsure, the sense of priorities will be skewed toward shortrange welfare objectives.

When should one sacrifice democratic process for authoritarian efficiency? In societies where the existence of a civic political culture is not the norm and where the agencies of central government inevitably play a crucial role in implementing development, the democratic process is often seen as a luxury which simply has to be postponed. Too much democracy, it is felt, leads to confusion among priorities, a lack of required discipline, a scattering of projects that are mutually inconsistent and unrealistic, and too much leverage given to collective ignorance rather than technical competence. There is limited confidence that the mass public actually knows what is good for it or that it is prepared to make intelligent choices. Worst of all, according to this view, the democratic system allows those opposed to development planning to engage in disruptive activity that easily exceeds the tolerance of an already fragile development effort.

Such thinking characterized the Indira Gandhi government in India during the mid-1970s. For example, in a question and answer session in Washington, the Indian Ambassador was challenged to explain why the Indian government was limiting freedom of the press. He argued that in the best of all possible worlds, their administration cherished a free press; they intended to have it. But at the moment the government faced the exceedingly difficult task—one of the most difficult in the world, he believed—of trying to meet the pressing, indeed, almost overwhelming needs of Indian society. It was not at all certain they would succeed. They simply could not afford any slippage in public confidence and coopera- tion. A free press had to take lower priority in India, where the press had traditionally stirred violent opposition to governmental re- gimes in the struggle for independence, where the political process was highly volatile, and where frequently the press, with few libel constraints, had been used as a tool for personal and political advantage. Gandhi could not allow the press to compromise government efforts for the common good. The American audience was not satisfied, but it was subdued. India faced a clear dilemma.

Thus, while Western advisors believe that development proj- ects will be most soundly based when they are democratically for- mulated and carried out, Third World developers may see democ- racy as an invitation to chaos. Some degree of benign authority makes common sense to them and to their constituent publics. The preference is often for an authoritarian regime, or even a totalitar- ian one in some cases, which will both ensure compliance with development plans and prohibit practices which stand in the way. Sometimes development appears to demand bold steps not likely to enjoy broad popular support. In countries like Indonesia, Bolivia and Tanzania, whole communities have been moved to new frontier areas of the country in the interest of a development plan. This kind of approach is standard in Communist development strategy. In India, many practices related to the caste system were simply prohibited by law. Singapore puts similar and seemingly arbitrary prohibitions on large families, as does the People's Re- public of China.

How do you strike a balance between revolution and peaceful change? To Western advisors, development through peaceful change is the proper objective. It suits their world view and value system and the Western world's vested interest in maintaining stability and predictability in international affairs. Where does this leave the Third World manager of development programs?

If one is already ideologically dedicated to democratic processes, that commitment may get the highest priority, even though change will be gradual. However, in many Third World situations, the developer who is dedicated to achieving real change may find the idea of a sudden and profound revolutionary solution persuasive. After living most of one's life in a static socio-economic system, one is likely to sense rather strongly that innovations and new programs will be diluted if simply introduced "democratically" into the system as it exists. That is, it is more likely that the system will blunt the innovations than that the innovations will change the system. The very nature of culture and of institutions is that they insure their own continuity, and the expectation that they will so perpetrate themselves becomes part of the mindset of the members of the society, whether they can articulate it or not. One simply knows that any real change will require breaking the mold: cutting the privileges of vested interests, destroying traditional institutions, forcing the mass of the populace to confront new ways of doing things. The outsider more often than not believes the new technique or project will be accepted on its own merits; the insider more easily perceives the system's resistance to change.

If development means changes in patterns of thinking, how can the media and communication resources be used effectively? Typically, in Third World countries communication resources are limited, and competition for their use is keen. Printing presses and newsprint are hard to obtain; readership is small and the ability to pay for newspapers and magazines frequently confined to a relatively small elite. The transistor revolution makes radios more available, but programming talent is often in short supply, leaving broadcast content to fall to the lowest levels of popular entertainment and advertising. Television is much more expensive, and broadcasting equipment and program production skills require major investment in capital and training. When TV is introduced, inexpensive foreign programming tends to fill many of the program hours. In short, the ability of the media to contribute to the public's education for development is uncertain at best; its content is likely to become an unguided missile as it introduces new ideas and information of questionable usefulness.

Media resources tend to receive major attention from Third World development planners. Uncontrolled, messages from the media can complicate their task of educating and forming values and outlooks consistent with the modernization process. On the other hand, the media can be very useful; it therefore seems to be too valuable a resource for development for any of it to be wasted. Thus, there may be considerable incentive for government and planning agencies to take over the media and to place heavy emphasis on development communication. When more sophisticated communication technology is available, it too is pressed into service for development objectives, as in the case of satellite-assisted television broadcasting. All this leaves the Western development advisor, especially the American, with mixed feelings. Employing new communication technology is an exciting prospect. But government domination of the media unnerves the Westerner and conjures up images of thought control: With only a little misdirection, the media can become an instrument of oppression in the service of authoritarianism.

Nevertheless, Third World interest in using the media for development purposes can be expected to continue and even be given a high priority. Both local media output and foreign programming and reporting may be monitored more carefully for their negative impact on changing local culture and values, and the preemption of communication systems for development objectives will probably be the trend for the near future.

The issues discussed above may suffice as evidence of the significance of mindsets to development affairs. Readers with experience in this field will think of further implications and applications. Perhaps some of the strongest evidence that the psychocultural dimension deserves closer attention is the fact that in real applications we find development schemes and projects always take longer than planned—if, indeed, they do not fall by the wayside altogether. The reason usually given is negative or complicating "political problems." This means, in final analysis, problems with mindsets.

CHAPTER SEVEN

Economic and Business Affairs

For the last application of our mindsets inquiry, let us turn briefly to mindsets that affect economic, business, and management affairs. We will only scratch the surface of a very large subject, but we can at least highlight a few of the more frequently recurring problem areas that the practitioner encounters in international work.

Superficially, it might seem that international differences in thinking and reasoning about economic and business matters would not be particularly significant. After all, commercial products, raw materials, money and credit, machinery, production equipment, transportation facilities, fuel and power, and the many technical services that are supplied internationally have a certain universal quality. They reflect human concerns and objectives that do not seem to differ fundamentally from place to place or from culture to culture. Economics addresses a world of tangible items that can be seen for what they are. They are subject to quantification; their values carry international price tags.

Consequently, international economic affairs have routinely been left to economists, who tend to pursue their analyses on the basis of that which can be quantified and entered into tested economic equations. Less tangible considerations, such as cultural factors that affect the way economic matters are perceived and understood, are given scant attention since they cannot be so easily quantified or factored into otherwise neat calculations and structured computer programs. Even the overriding impact of unquantifiable contrasts in economic ideology often tends to be skirted, ignored or categorized as a political-economic variable and, therefore, another discipline. Not surprisingly, the practice of "hard" economic analysis often leaves us short of dependable explanations for how economic forces actually operate, and certainly far short of reliable guidelines for anticipating what will actually happen in managing international economic affairs. In fact the track record of international economists is not very impressive.

The problem is that so-called "scientific" economic analysis ordinarily assumes those involved in economic activity will act "rationally," that *everything else being equal*, people will make economic decisions on the basis of their economic self-interest. Such analysis necessarily omits all the other things that are *not* equal, and leaves them to judgment based on experience or the analytical talents of other disciplines. An interdisciplinary approach to international economic processes hardly exists. Most important, routine applications of conventional economic analysis cannot tolerate "irrational" behavior. But, from a cross-national and cross-cultural perspective, there is a real question as to what is rational and what irrational; both are very relative terms and very much culture bound; one person's irrationality might turn out to be another's orderly and predictable behavior.

We do not want to overstate the case. Actually, much international business and negotiation does proceed in a "rational," economically predictable manner, and there is a degree of international uniformity in making economic choices. At the present stage of history, one can even think of an internationalized "super-culture" underlying the mainstream of economic activity. A recognized commonality of assumptions and expectations exists for dealing with an international system in which everything from steel to television programming to hotel accommodations and airline tickets "flows" in an international market. Along with this there is a global banking culture which includes an internationally accepted system of laws and regulations that governs most financial obligations and performance. So we know, and expect, that most of the time our international economic machinery will operate without great concern for variations in the cultural and psychological dimension.

But that is *most* of the time, and for the more routine and repetitive economic processes. Many of our most crucial and demanding economic problems defy any internationally shared common sense. After all, managers and policy makers do have to anticipate political realities, differing perceptions of economic issues, and perhaps the "irrationality" of a Third World charismatic leader. Even Europeans have to cope with what they see as "irrationality" among themselves as they try to make the Common Market work. On occasion, economic boycotts are used as instruments of international policy, sometimes as substitutes for stronger military action. All this is not very neat as economic science, but it is very real when economic outcomes have to be calculated.

Many of the world's most important economic events have reflected noneconomic mindsets. The formation of OPEC (Organization of Petroleum Exporting Countries) and the dramatic price increase in oil it imposed on the rest of the world was motivated in large part by noneconomic concerns. It was a way to gain leverage to achieve ends beyond profiting from oil. Especially in the Middle East, there was a feeling that the international community had suddenly tilted again toward Israel. Other OPEC countries had other grievances. All felt they had been taken for granted too long and wanted to be seen as something more important than just the world's oil field. Subsequently, OPEC's inability to surmount internal rivalries and animosities and to function cohesively as a group produced another round of far-reaching economic consequences as oil prices fell. Noneconomic and even emotional preoccupations often motivate nationalization of foreign investments, sometimes flying in the face of "objective" self-interest. Economic affairs can include events arising almost entirely from noneconomic concerns, as when Coca Cola is attacked not for its qualities as a product, or for its price, but for the idea that it represents "cultural imperialism."

Even in routine business and management affairs unanticipated mindsets can throw projects off track. I recall an American highway construction firm working in Bolivia that had to ask the local National Guard to break up an armed siege of one of its remote construction camps where American supervisors were being held at bay by their own local employees. It was not wages or working conditions that had brought the project to a halt, but mostly an efficient but impersonal American management style which clashed with the employees' sense of personal dignity.

Undiagnosed social and psycho-cultural factors played a crucial role in the series of events that led up to the international debt crisis of the mid-1980s. Many Third World countries had accumulated obligations beyond their ability to repay. They could not even continue to pay interest if they were to resolve their mounting internal economic and political problems. What had gone wrong? How had the genius of modern international economic science wandered into such a mess? As the loan policies and projects of both public and private lenders were conceived over the years, a conventional wisdom among the lenders had assumed that investment in human resources and in a series of infrastructure projects such as roads, hydroelectric projects and local financial institutions would produce the kind of expanded economies in the Third World that would make repayment relatively easy; at least that is how it worked in the model of development followed by the countries now doing the lending. But as the projects were started and debts accumulated, the expected growth that would enable the borrowers to repay the loans did not take place. Too many noneconomic factors came into play, factors which did not mesh with the assumptions and mindsets by which the loans were urged upon these countries in the first place. Political pressures and problems that political leaders had to attend to often derailed development project priorities. Polarized Third World social systems did not provide the same incentives for utilizing capital and infrastructure investments as anticipated by First World planners. And there were psycho-cultural factors ranging from outlooks on work and productivity to patterns of trust, accountability, and responsibility at the national level that impinged on economic performance.

In the management field, we have already mentioned the differing American and Japanese management styles and the cultural assumptions on which contrasts are based. Similar and even greater management mindset problems arise in the Middle East. Petroleum income has been used for vast modernization projects—airports, water systems, communication facilities, new planned cities—that depend on foreign technical supervision and even foreign construction workers. These projects are ultra-modern, but assumptions deriving from traditional Islamic society lead to conceptions of management which are not easily bridged by engineers and business executives. Simply understanding who has the authority to make decisions and what the rationale is for making those decisions poses a distinct challenge.

Among international investors it is becoming increasingly common practice to include some kind of risk analysis in investment planning, the "risk" being precisely the threat posed by mindset and other factors that seem "irrational" in projections of operating costs or investment security. Even large and experienced international banks make costly, even disastrous mistakes, as we noted above, in relation to their role in the Third World debt crisis.

The demand for skills in anticipating contrasting mindset and reasoning factors in international business will increase, especially as growing interdependence converts a larger portion of domestic business operations into some form of international business and as the sheer economic leverage of countries previously outside the decision-making mainstream of international economic affairs is felt. Mexico, Taiwan, Korea, and India are now central actors; however, their view of the issues is often culturally unique and not always easily understood by technical economists or narrowly experienced policy makers, governmental or private.

Communicating about economic problems is becoming increasingly complicated by the highly abstract nature of international economic institutions. Consider the abstruse thinking that goes into government economic policies, or into calculating long-range financial projections, designing the investment and production projects undertaken by multinational corporations, or balancing advantage and benefits in the international monetary system. And in economics, as in the fields we discussed earlier, the more abstract the subject matter, the more important the mindset which governs how it is pursued. It is one thing to achieve a meeting of minds when selling barrels of petroleum or bushels of wheat. It is another matter when the subject is a joint venture to produce a manufactured product or to contract for managerial services. The first can be conceptualized rather directly; the latter has to exist at least partly in mental images and constructs. Therefore, the more intricate the problem at hand and the greater the contrast in culture and national society, the more difficult it will be to anticipate the direction of a foreign counterpart's reasoning.

In the face of all these hard-to-grasp complications, the temptation to stick to manipulating quantified data in the analysis and management of economic affairs is strong and grows stronger as the potential for computer processing increases in attractiveness by giving the data and the conclusions drawn from it an aura of infallibility. Unfortunately, the computer can only process quantifiable data that fits into the models incorporated in its software programs, while the real world of economic processes includes all the unanticipated factors that resist sterile quantification.

The purpose of this chapter, then, is to discuss several of the kinds of contrasts in mindsets that make a significant difference in the way economic processes are understood and handled around the world. The following is not a body of economic theory, but an attempt to call more attention to an aspect of diagnosing international economic interaction that is too often insufficiently regarded. Four such areas for exploring differences have been selected:

1. Outlooks on the basic elements of economic activity, such as value placed on work and productivity, goods and services, commercial activity, managing people and resources, and saving and investing.

2. The varying ways that social structure, resulting perceptual systems, and economic activity are interrelated.

3. The way a society's social philosophy, including formal ideology, provides its members with underlying assumptions about the social purpose of their economic institutions.

4. The impact of public images and beliefs regarding the operation of the international economic system.

VALUE ASSUMPTIONS IN THINKING ABOUT ECONOMIC MATTERS

Work, saving money, production, trade, and resource management are basic elements in any economy. If societies differ in fundamental beliefs about these elements, or value them in varying ways, then the stage is set at the start for diverse conceptions of the nature of economic systems. The following example of two ways of thinking about work illustrates the problem and the function of values.

A Latin American friend once suggested to me that I could better understand U.S.-Latin American business relations by analyzing the subjective meaning of the words that are used in English and Spanish. In English, the word "business" is positive. It connotes "busyness," doing things—and that is good. One is going about one's business, is getting down to business, is responsible for attending to one's work responsibilities; one is *not* loafing or pursuing pleasure before the business at hand is completed. It is the normal and right condition of life. In Spanish, the word is "negocio." Here, he suggested, the value is turned around. The key is the "ocio" part of the word, which connotes leisure, serenity, time to enjoy and contemplate as the preferred human condition and circumstance. But when harsh reality forces one from one's "ocio," when it is negated, then one has to attend to "negocio." The subjective meaning is obviously much less positive than in English.

Conclusions from this linguistic comparison should not be overdrawn; the immediate meaning is clear enough. Still, the latent meaning which reflects differences in the values that a society applies to business is significant. The Latin American conception of the worth of the "public man," as noted in Chapter Three, is consistent with this. It suggests a culture-specific type of "achievement motivation" that leads one to perceive work, business, entrepreneurship, priority given to a business routine, and the like, in a manner quite different from the way they are perceived in English-speaking countries. The Anglo-Saxon folk wisdom that "the devil finds work for idle hands" makes no sense.

Are some societies, because of their hierarchy of values, more materialistic than others? "Materialism" is not easily defined or compared, but the question is: Will some cultures lead people to direct their energies more happily toward some form of material gain or accomplishment, or toward another kind of goal which is spiritual, artistic, or humanistic? Do all people engage in their materialistic pursuits with the same inventiveness or single-mindedness of purpose? Do material possessions, or skills in producing and distributing material products, confer the same prestige? Are such measures of "success"? Is there a basic value placed on science or on applied knowledge so that conquering the material world is in itself a source of satisfaction?

While at first blush it may seem that these questions are more appropriate in addressing differences among individual tastes and life styles, it is evident that such economic predispositions do vary cross-culturally. The questions are fundamental in projects involving technological transfer or in development, as noted in the last chapter. They also apply more broadly in seeking to understand variations in the rationale different people and cultures have for economic activity.

Different cultures define and value work itself in distinctive ways. It may be considered an unpleasant burden to be borne, or a duty, or a positive good as in the Protestant Ethic, where it is placed on a pedestal. But in any case, how it is conceived will have far-reaching effects on the functioning of an economic system. The Japanese cannot be said to have a "Protestant" Ethic, but work there does enjoy a high social status in the web of belonging, of duty and obligation that characterizes Japanese social relations. An achievement motif is clearly present. Perhaps in some socialistic societies group achievement goals take the place of the individualistic achievement motivations found in capitalistic countries. In traditional societies work is likely to be seen as fate and therefore unavoidable. Although no alternatives to work are expected, no positive value is assigned to it either.

The point is that the motivating mindset for work itself varies cross-culturally, and corresponding value orientations need to be considered in anticipating the way that work issues will be perceived cross-nationally. As a society's mass work base constitutes the drive chain of its economic system, psycho-cultural explanations of *why* it operates as it does in a given place is a key element in understanding a country's economic dynamics.

Rewards for work, or punishments for not working, are also culturally determined, and of course are a function of the particular economic system. The work motivation that simply keeps one from slipping over the edge of marginal survival is quite different from a motivation that seeks direct rewards in higher levels of material or social well-being. If such a direct relationship is uncertain or missing, then the worker might turn attention to alternatives such as luck and good fortune, to lotteries, or the beneficence of God or of the government. Such outlooks, again, affect the psychological basis for economic productivity.

Societies and culture groups also differ in the value placed on trading and on commercial activity, and indeed in the degree to which the social and cultural system itself is based on trade and commerce. Overseas Chinese are notorious for their trading skills. The merchants of Venice left their mark on Italian culture of that era. In American society there is a pervasive emphasis on the distribution of goods as evidenced in the omnipresence of supermarkets and shopping malls. In the functioning of economic systems, this kind of commercial activity results not simply from an occupational emphasis but also from a state of mind. Conversely, such a state of mind would be lacking in a subsistence economy where members of the society may not perceive their economic activity within the context of a monetary system at all.

Modern economic performance is significantly affected by the way ownership of capital and other resources is organized. How cultures lead their practitioners to think about such things as private property, land, money, and ownership is fundamental to the cross-cultural analysis of economic behavior. Some discussion of this subject will come later in relation to the social purpose of economic institutions. Here, as a matter of values and patterns of thinking, it is important to note that great differences exist in the degree to which money and capital resources are thought of as something that can be *cumulative* and enduring over time rather than as resources for meeting immediate needs and desires. This perspective varies, to be sure, with styles of reasoning which may or may not associate today's purposive actions with a distant tomorrow's consequences—the difference between "waste not, want not" and "que será, será," or "if God wills."

In the United States New Englanders are traditionally known for their moral stance in using and accumulating capital, managing it wisely, and not dipping into it for frivolous purposes. Capital has a sanctity; one feels a sense of responsibility for its safekeeping; prestige goes with husbanding it carefully. In contrast, the ordinary Filipino has traditionally lived in a world where it is the present that is real, not the future, and where today's concerns take priority in the use of available assets. Because the Chinese community in the Philippines handles resources with a concrete sense of future purpose, they have come to play a vital role in capital accumulation and in owning and operating many of the enterprises on which the overall economy depends. A real dilemma arises when, despite Chinese discretion in avoiding ostentation that will bring reprisals, their obvious advantage sets off nationalistic resentment and government attempts to curb their domination. Their culturally-sustained mode of operation is essential to the economy because an alternative source of local investment capital is not available; disciplined saving is not very strongly supported psycho-culturally by the Filipino value system. While the Philippine economy is a highly complex system that includes Spanish, American and Japanese influences among others, the development of a cultural base conducive to modern economic investment performance continues to be a matter of significant concern among Filipino economists.

Culture-based mindsets also affect stock markets. The willingness to invest in impersonal financial institutions requires certain assumptions, not only about how one uses money and assets in the first place, but about the confidence needed to risk investment with strangers—a psychologically loaded proposition. Thus, investment accumulation through the issuance of stocks and bonds requires a special feeling of public confidence in the impersonal integrity and enduring health of the institutions in question. It also requires faith that the national system, including the government, will be stable and predictable over time. It has been argued that industrial development in Latin America has progressed slowly because Latin Americans with resources for investment have tended to have more confidence in financial institutions *outside* their own countries than inside; their assets go to finance enterprises in Europe or in the United States instead of at home. Investment within Latin America has more often flowed into channels of existing confidence, for example, family corporations, or into investments that will pay off quickly, as in short-term commercial ventures, apartment houses, casinos, or the like. This is not irrational economic behavior by any means. If one cannot be sure what kind of government will be in place, what laws will be in force, what economic policies will be pursued, or what the value of the local currency will be some distance into the future, resources will go into consumption, personal property, or investments with a short fuse. In this context, the successful operation of modern stock exchanges in developing societies constitutes more of a radical and fundamental change than the outsider might appreciate, for that success represents a sharp change in the underlying mentality by which people invest. Because of the lack of confidence needed to draw private resources into long-range capital investment, governments often feel compelled to become the investor of choice in large and long-term projects.

Banking itself is, in the final analysis, a state of mind as well as a complex of laws and institutionalized services. As was suggested earlier, one's expectations of banking institutions and one's reasons for using them will differ. In terms of mindsets, a Swiss bank is not the same as an American bank, or an English or Brazilian bank. In many societies, a bank is not considered a suitable guardian of one's assets; owning land or gold gives more assurance.

I recall an example of banking mindsets from eastern Bolivia. A disastrous flood in Cochabamba had leveled some 200 adobe houses. (When the water level reached the first layer of adobe bricks, they disintegrated; the houses slowly descended into a mass of mud.) Among other relief resources, limited USAID funds were made available to the flood area for loans to experiment with new kinds of improved housing for low-income victims. As principal officer of the Consulate, I was approached by two brothers, not affected by the flood, who wanted to borrow from this fund. What they had in mind was a new house considerably outside the intentions of the project, so they were told it would not be possible. When I asked why they did not simply borrow from a bank, they protested that this was very expensive with interest at 6% or 7%. As that compared favorably with U.S. mortgages, I said those rates did not seem unreasonable to me. But, they said, I did not understand—it was 6% a month! The very idea of extending loans to ordinary citizens for long periods of time was foreign to local thinking. Somewhat later, when the First National City Bank of New York came into Cochabamba, bringing with it all the expectations of American banking, it was a culture shock, both to local citizens and local banks. While the enterprise did seem to gain ground with local clients, in the end it was maneuvered out by the Bolivian banking community because its operating rationale was indigestible in the context of Bolivian tradition.

Despite the frequent assertion that sentimentality and the pursuit of economic interests don't mix, economic systems are in fact ethical systems. Whether by law and regulation or by custom, some economic activities are sanctioned while others are not. And what is sanctioned differs from culture to culture. This has much to do with the way that economic actions and events are perceived and reacted to and the way decisions are made. Management systems are also ethical systems; what is comfortably accepted and tolerable in one culture may not be in another. While such a fundamental concept as competition might be seen as a positive good in some societies, supported by the idea of fair play as discussed above, it is viewed as a source of chaos and inefficiency in others.

In any case most economic activity rests on well-established norms for complying with agreements for delivering goods, paying bills, performing according to contracts, adhering to standards, etc. In much of the West, these norms are embodied in precise written and legal contracts. Confidence is derived from adherence to these norms. Thus, the extraordinary dependence on contract law, the courts, lawyers, and insurance to protect against liabilities that come with the system. Mutual obligations are *legal* obligations; disputes are subject to *legal* interpretation of contractual arrangements.

This is not so much the case in Japan, where the ratio of lawyers to the population is low (at least ten times lower than in the U.S.). Among the Japanese the existence of established honorable relationships and a stated intent to comply makes exact contracts less essential. This approach allows the Japanese to make changes and adjustments as conditions and circumstances require without technical contractual revisions, a practice which Americans may interpret as deviousness or evidence of questionable intentions in the first place. To the Japanese, reliance on a formal contract is unfortunate for it suggests a mutual lack of honor. They tend to fall back on the contract only as a remedy of last resort.

This conflict in economic mindset can affect economic performance more than one might suppose. Once, in an American-Japanese debate regarding relative advantage in production costs, the Japanese claimed that they spent much less on "confidence." They suggested that Americans should calculate the high price paid for confidence through time and effort spent in negotiating complex contracts, hiring expensive lawyers, taking out costly insurance, and engaging in unnecessary lawsuits—none of which contribute to productivity. If, indeed, the Japanese do manage to hold down these kinds of costs, then it is certainly one area in which the American competitive edge is being lost.

On the other hand, where societies lack a culture-based pattern of establishing confidence—whether through concepts of honor and consensus or a system of practical and binding law—or where law and sanctioned practice are in conflict, there may be an inadequate confidence base for any kind of modern economic system to work.

SOCIAL STRUCTURES, PERCEPTUAL SYSTEMS, AND ECONOMIC ACTIVITY

In sociological studies a society's social structure is usually considered a function of its economic system. Indeed, the economic system is often seen as a basic explanation for patterns of social relationships; in the Marxist view, it is virtually the single factor. Social status and social classes are often defined in terms of wealth and influence in the system. More rigorous sociological analysis goes much beyond this, to be sure, but it is standard practice to judge economic issues in terms of relative advantage for various subdivisions in the hierarchy of society—classes, ethnic groups, etc.

If we want to compare the way specific economic events or issues are perceived *internationally*, we might ask how thinking about economic matters is determined by position and vested interest in the social structures in question. Differing social structures will create different economic mindsets. For example, a British labor union, whose members are socialized in a society somewhat more tightly structured than in the U.S., will react differently to a government proposal to nationalize an industry than an American union would. Among other factors, they might be more interested as a group in the powers of government because they see their political intervention as a social class better advancing their interests. Union members in the U.S. tend to be more individualistic, seeing personal initiative and mobility as a better means of getting ahead, even if it does not always work out that way. American union members might own stock in the company that employs them, or they may think of eventually going into business on their own. The difference may be small, but it is real, and the consequence is that American union members, in contrast to their British brothers, tend to be very suspicious of government control of industry.

From an international perspective, the economic mindsets that stem from the dominance of the middle class in American society are rather exceptional. A highly individualistic, self-reliant, achievement-oriented population in which everyone hopes to advance in status and relative advantage forms the psychological foundation for an economy in which people across the board invest in securities, value personal initiative and are willing to assume responsibilities in the workplace. This social outlook has generated a mass consumer market and the advertising practices that go with it. All this sets the stage for the positive role that competition plays in a free enterprise environment. It also helps one understand the

American attitude toward work and even makes logical all the do-it-yourself activity for which Americans are famous.

The psychological stage is set very differently in more stratified societies. Individuals do not internalize the same conception of themselves, of their potential, or of the desirability of applying individual initiative. Obviously, the accompanying economic system will have to operate with a logic consistent with the mindsets of that kind of social psychology. In such societies, an elite or even an economic aristocracy—perhaps people that go back to a landowning class—may fill the roles that the achievement-oriented, upwardly mobile executive does in the American system. Labor leaders may need to be politicians first to promote the cause of their constituents, rather than the entrepreneur-oriented organizers found in labor organizations in middle-class American society. A servant segment of the society might be a significant element in the economy. The market for consumer goods would reflect the consumption habits and buying potential of that public. As a practical example of a difference due to social structure, Sears stores in the United States cater to middle—and even lower-middle-class customers. In Mexico, where Sears has also been very successful, it is a store for the elite and new middle classes.

To the extent that new middle sector groups are developing in changing societies, the potential, for operating a successful free enterprise system as known in the United States increases. Conversely, as the population in the U.S. becomes more dense and the frontier ethos fades further into the past, it becomes more probable that the system will be modified by more regulation to reflect the needs of what is in fact a less open and mobile society.

The mindsets that go with differing social systems also have to be taken into account in cross-cultural management practices. Consider, for example, the case of Japanese companies opening factories in the United States. Many have attempted to structure their operations according to Japanese management concepts, which assume employees have a more group-oriented outlook and need to feel a stronger sense of belonging and of being mutually committed with management to the achievement of company objectives than is usual for American employees. In the U.S. a more impersonal set of individual-to-company relationships pervades the working environment. This attempt to adapt Japanese managerial styles to the American work setting has been interesting.

Individualistic Americans often resist or resent singing the company song or engaging in group calisthenics as is the custom in Japanese companies, and American executives may object to allowing their authority to be diffused in a Japanese consensus-type operation. Yet, American workers tend to respond favorably to the Japanese manager's concern for their personal worth and the degree to which their ideas about company operations are sought and appreciated, things that are frequently absent in the impersonal operation of the American factory system.

Or note another example which goes the other way. In this case American managers abroad projected on local employees their implicit assumptions regarding motivation, individualism, and personal independence. The case involved an American petroleum company not long after it had established operations in Venezuela. The question pertained to housing for local executive and managerial personnel. As was the custom there, the company supplied company housing as part of its total package of personnel benefits. The Americans felt, however, that this housing arrangement was overly paternalistic, that it was demeaning and engendered more of a sense of dependence than their employees would find dignified. They therefore took what they felt was an enlightened and progressive step and set up a financial plan by which the employees could purchase their homes at very favorable terms and thus gain a greater degree of self-respect and sense of independence. The initial reaction from the Venezuelans, however, was negative—not what the Americans had anticipated. The resistance, it turned out, stemmed from a feeling that *not* having company housing increased the sense of distance and impersonal relationship between the company and local managerial personnel and decreased the company's commitment to them as special persons. Their sense of security in the company was threatened. They *liked* the paternalism implied by the company housing; it made them feel they belonged.

The fact that most societies are more rigidly structured than American society is economically significant. In other cultures the right of an economic elite to enjoy advantages is usually more acceptable, as are the relatively modest circumstances of other sectors of society. Or it may be that getting ahead in a more stratified system involves a "common sense assumption" that one's entire social group or class will have to get ahead (as seen, to a degree, in the case of British labor cited above). The stratified society thus encourages competition for advantage more among groups than among individuals. In extreme situations an individual's aspiration to rise from a lowly status might be considered unreasonable, if not somewhat odd; and to feel failure because one has not risen to the top would be bizarre indeed. This psychological mindset is more congenial to the logic of socialist economies as far as furthering individual well-being is concerned. From this vantage point, free enterprise is often seen as creating more of an environment for exploitation than for individual advantage.

The new middle-class groups that do emerge in more tightly structured societies thus occupy the middle ground socially but find that they inherit a culture that has not provided the middle-class roles, values and expectations that would supply identity, self-esteem and a sense of purpose for them. They have, in effect, moved into a kind of cultural vacuum. In many developing countries, what one often sees is a psycho-cultural struggle in which people are attempting to adapt old values and create new ones appropriate to a modern middle class in a society that never had a middle-class culture before.

WHAT IS THE IMPLICIT SOCIAL PURPOSE OF ECONOMIC INSTITUTIONS?

International economic dialogue is often plagued by the fact that institutions which at face value seem to be strictly economic in nature—an international airline, for example—defy ordinary economic logic. The rationale for the existence of the institution in any given case may be skewed toward some noneconomic social concern or national preoccupation. The national airline of a country may lose money, but it does carry the flag abroad, and that can be reason enough for its existence, with economic considerations, as such, secondary. Often, understanding economic institutions in another country is a matter of capturing the sense of social and political priorities surrounding them. These priorities can vary enormously from one culture and set of circumstances to another. Thus the seriousness of the question: *What is the implicit social purpose of a given economic activity?*

Social purpose, which is studied most by sociologists, is both the basis for ideological persuasions and an underlying element in the thinking of economic policy planners. Assumptions about society constitute key factors in Keynesian and Marxian theories, just as they do in the more recently formulated supply-side economics of the Reagan era. And a sense of social purpose also becomes an integral part of the public's conventional wisdom as people go about their ordinary economic activity. All this commands a vast literature in many languages, and one will not get far in comparing the logic of economic systems without delving into it.

Here we will rather pragmatically confine the discussion to a few selected areas in which differences in the way people consciously or unconsciously define social purposes repeatedly come up: ownership and property, profit making, and taxation.

Ownership and property. The social purpose and meaning of ownership and property are fundamental parts of the rationale of any economic system, be it the ownership of land, underground minerals, communications systems, public utilities, heavy industry, copyrights, or even other human beings at some stages of history— the list is endless. But ownership is comprehensible only in the context of the social and cultural system (and its values), which answers such questions as: *What* can be owned? *Who* can own it? And to *what purpose?* In terms of the logic of cultural systems, the latter question is the more basic; the sense of purpose embedded in the culture will tend to determine the what and who.

Around the world we find property owned variously by nations, kings, religious institutions, corporations, families, and individuals. In the U.S. it has even been bequeathed to cats and dogs! Much depends on the value emphasis of the society, especially, as discussed earlier, whether that emphasis is on the individual or on the group.

If the culture places the group first, then obviously the social purpose of property is to serve the interests of the group, and those interests will logically put limits on private ownership. Thus, it might not seem reasonable to leave ownership of and control over property to the caprice of private individuals whose purposes might be too narrow for group well-being. Again, this mindset is characteristic of socialist approaches to national economics.

If the *individual* comes first, then the logic of free enterprise and a capitalistic society falls into place. The rationalization is that in the long run, the free choice exercised by individuals in deciding how they take advantage of their ownership will benefit everyone. Accordingly, the individual is given considerable license to use property in ways that would be seen as antisocial in places where group priorities demand that limits be placed both on *what* can be owned and *who* can own it.

The social purpose of property often becomes the issue in social revolution; it may be so crucial a concern that determination to change a social order translates into a demand for fast and dramatic changes in land ownership, in foreign ownership and control of local resources, or the imposition of upper limits on the accumulation of wealth. Reviewing the various revolutionary movements of recent history—China, Mexico, Russia, Nicaragua— makes this clear, of course. However, "revolution" goes on in milder forms in many other places, including Western industrial countries, as conditions such as population density or the "explosion of rising expectations" change the sense of social purpose surrounding property and ownership. Economic thinking in the U.S. took a sharp turn in the 1930s when the Roosevelt administration provided the country with a new definition of social purpose and set it off on a new track of economic logic.

Profit-making. Profit as a matter of social purpose is closely related to ownership. The free enterprise system assumes that profit is the incentive that both drives economic performance and makes it rational. From this point of view, individual initiative, rewards for productivity, and the accumulation of capital make sense. The dilemma posed is that profit can become an end in itself, so that the economic system tends to encourage the pursuit of activity that results in profit but which does not produce goods or services. To some observers, the American fixation on profit is a threat to the international economic system for just that reason. Even within the U.S., we are coming to debate the economic function of nonproductive profit creation, such as we see in the increasing wave of stock manipulations, corporate mergers, leveraged buyouts, and opportunistic lawsuits that go beyond reasonable justice to pursue whatever profit the traffic will bear, all of which seems to prostitute the free enterprise system and to contradict its supposed basic social purposes.[1]

Japan presents a subtle variation on the logic of both ownership and profit. Gene Gregory, of Sophia University in Tokyo, stresses that national economic survival has been a salient societal motive since Japan began to industrialize following the Meiji restoration. Taking this into account, it should not be surprising to learn that Japanese "private enterprise" differs markedly in its logic from both European and American economic systems. It is not so "private," or at least not so geared to serve private purposes as it is to serve national and social ones, that is, the common good. In this perspective, the often discussed close relationship between large industries and the Japanese Ministry of International Trade and Industry (MITI) makes sense. Also, private and public ownership tend to blend in definition; ownership becomes something more of a public trust. Aggressive profit-seeking is somewhat less the point than is the careful managing of scarcities which allows for achieving the highest production with available resources. In this system, efficiency and a highly educated work force become the means for national survival. Labor and management share more of a common goal, more of an agreed sense of social purpose in any given industrial institution.[2]

Social purpose may lead societies to sanction profit in one activity and not another. In the United States, for example, it seems only common sense that the institutions gathering and distributing the news should be profit-making entities. By this logic, the consumer is in charge, competition is healthy, and news flow is sealed off from government control—which is seen as evil. In other countries news flow is believed to be too important to be left to a profit-making organization; it is the responsibility of government to manage the gathering and dissemination of news, to keep its citizens informed. Thus, the debate over a "New International Information Order," which has raged in recent years between Third World and Western nations, is based in some degree on quite different conceptions of the relationship between news and social purpose.

While news is in the domain of private business in the U.S., education is seen as the responsibility of government or of non-profit institutions. Social purpose demands that priority be given to educating without regard to ability to pay; this fits the American image of the good society. Americans are disturbed when they find that in the Philippines large numbers of institutions of higher learning are profit-making private enterprises. The conclusion from the U.S. cultural perspective: News is a commercial product, education is not. It is not very productive to expect these perspectives—or, in our terminology here, mindsets—to be universal or absolute.

Taxation. The social meaning of taxation, like the issues raised above, is the direct result of the way people perceive their reciprocal obligation with their government and the degree to which citizens personally identify with the nation as a whole. It is on the basis of these kinds of feelings that personal compliance with tax laws is obtained.

The U.S. personal income tax is relatively unique in that, for the most part, people *assume* that they should and will pay. The system is largely unpoliced, and it works. Its success, however, is relatively fragile, for it is based on mindsets and patterns of thinking that can be undermined if the value orientations that go with it are violated. When tax avoidance through the use of loopholes and other abuses becomes widespread, taxation appears unfair, and the basis for unquestioned compliance is eroded, as was recognized in the 1986 tax reform. It is eroded too when leaders who are expected to sustain the value by example evade their own taxes. Former President Nixon's tax adventures are a case in point. It is interesting to note that his attempt to manipulate tax advantages was not seen as terribly important in a number of other countries where paying taxes is less of a moral imperative. American indignation was not easily understood.

The problem of matching the tax system to the culture can be seen in another Philippine example, one particularly poignant since so much effort went into planting the American economic system in the Philippines during the era of American administration of the islands. In the early 1960s, when it was obvious that the Philippine government's tax system was functioning inadequately to support development efforts, the U.S. technical assistance program brought in a team of American Internal Revenue Service consultants to advise. At about this time a national election campaign was heating up in the Philippines, and the press was reporting a scandal in which a Senator had evaded most of his taxes the year before. He had paid only about the equivalent of $400, yet he was known for his wealth in landholdings, banking, interisland shipping, etc. While en route to an appointment, an American consultant asked his taxi driver what he thought of the Senator's paying $400 in income taxes. The answer: "Oh, that is all right, sir, he can afford it." Could it be that the common sense assumption held by the public was one that did not expect ordinary people to actually pay personal income taxes?

In many countries, especially in the developing world, the approach taken to taxation is different. Taxes are levied so that the government does not have to depend on the individual's tax ethic. Taxes are levied instead on such things as imports, especially luxury goods. In this way, those who can afford to pay, will pay. Or when possible, taxes are levied on exports. Thus, government can pay for the public welfare from the public's assets. In any case, who pays and how much is socially and culturally a very relative matter.

This question of social purpose and meaning can be directed to many other key elements of an economic system: investing, credit, welfare, urban planning and so forth. The payoff is that this kind of analysis calls attention to reasons for differences in economic structuring and variations in performance from one culture to another in what otherwise might be seen to be similar economic entities. Probing social purpose may establish a rationale that might not otherwise be evident.

PUBLIC IMAGES OF THE INTERNATIONAL ECONOMIC SYSTEM

As a final section of this chapter, we will consider the kaleidoscope of mindsets by which the international economic system itself is perceived. In a world ever more tightly drawn together and interconnected in its economic processes, the pressure increases for an international economic system that operates with some degree of multinational consensus. Trends such as the growth of multinational corporations that operate with a kind of practical worldwide rationality on the one hand, and demands for a new international economic order on the other, demonstrate the quest for a more coherent system. Perhaps the greatest challenge to mindset analysis comes when one attempts to apply it to all the ways the international economic system itself is viewed and understood—to all the images and beliefs about it.

This multiplicity of views rests in part on differences in ideology and sense of social purpose, as noted above. It also reflects vastly differing experience with the international system and national position within it. Industrialized societies competing for supremacy in high technology fields carry very different preoccupations into their thinking about the international economic system as compared to societies still seeking a transition from colonialism and the dependency psychology that goes with it.

A number of specific variations in views vital to the way the international system functions call for closer examination.

First in importance, perhaps, is the matter of the role governments are expected to play in international economic affairs, particularly in contrast to the role of private economic institutions. For example, as Japan and the United States negotiate their interrelationship, the American negotiating load is carried more purposefully by the private industries involved, with the Departments of Commerce and State responding more to regulatory problems than carrying the initiative. In Japan, the government Ministry of International Trade and Industry coordinates both government and private industrial positions and strategies.

The economics of the international airline industry is another case in point. In some countries the airlines are private; in others they are government owned, or at least subsidized. Thus, governments negotiating regulations start with very different views of their roles. To compound the problem of government versus private policy making, we note that the present international system includes governments whose prime mission is to control totally their domestic economy, as in Communist countries. There are also governments committed to exercising the least control possible, and even some, historically, that were themselves under the control of the economic enterprises. International economic issues are viewed by the various nations accordingly.

This multiplicity of expected government roles poses difficulties for world-level economic institutions such as the International Monetary Fund and the many regulatory agencies of the United Nations which serve a multinational constituency. The problem is that while these supranational institutions have formal charters and regulations, they are not institutionalized in the mindsets of their clients in the sense that the people of the various countries involved share mental pictures of what these institutions are and how they should function. Differing regional and local expectations are thus projected at the start onto the roles played both by international organizations and the national governments dealing with them. All of this makes agreement on and execution of international programs an extremely discordant exercise.

The United States, for example, would find it difficult to

cooperate in an international agreement regarding regulation of international television broadcasting. Its philosophy would dictate as little regulation as possible in the first place, and its constitution would permit little control over the information and entertainment enterprises of its citizens in the second. More authoritarian countries, on the other hand, would be likely to see regulation as more desirable and natural and would have little trouble enforcing it. Hence the built-in difference in the way issues are perceived in international organizations, whatever the subject matter being addressed.

Values and Notions of Justice and Equity. The most fundamental issue in considering images and expectations involves the sense of justice and equity by which the international system works. The so-called North-South divergence in economic views is a case in point. The nations of the southern part of the globe see themselves as economically dependent and politically powerless, subject to continuous exploitation or some form of economic colonialism. They see the evidence of this condition in international economic agreements, in the flow of goods, in the operation of multinational corporations, in prices paid for raw materials in contrast to those asked for manufactured goods, etc. Obviously, there is in reality much to substantiate this view, but it is the view itself that is the mindset consideration and needs to be taken into account.

The following is an example of the problem. An Ecuadorean complained during a discussion that there seemed no way out of a situation in which the prices that Ecuadorean producers received for a box of bananas at dockside in Ecuador was only 10% of the price for which it eventually sold in U.S. supermarkets. He noted that if the Ecuadoreans tried to add just a few cents to their price, buyers would simply turn to Central America. To him, this was calculated unfairness, economic imperialism.

This seemed an exaggeration to me, so as Ecuadorean desk officer in the State Department at that time, I checked it out. What he said was quite true. Almost 90% of the final price went to the cost of loading at the dock, shipping to Panama, Panama Canal charges, shipping to New Orleans, off-loading there at high labor costs, transportation to a wholesale center in Kentucky where shipments were subdivided for final destinations, further handling and shipping by truck or rail, distribution to the local supermarket chain, cost of retailing, insurance and, finally, credit. All along the way there were fixed costs regardless of the value of the original product. The grower was in perhaps the worst bargaining position of anyone in the chain. Bananas have only a short life span, and if they are not sold quickly, they are a total loss. Still, it was difficult to find *calculated* exploitation. Nonetheless, the overall system would remain unfair unless the banana growers, like petroleum producers later, could cooperate to force up minimum prices for the raw product.

Growers maintain that even doubling their price would make relatively little difference in the final cost. But the government in the U.S. would hesitate to intervene to help Ecuadorean growers as it prefers to leave the solution of such problems to private enterprise, where no compelling problem is seen, and there are no American banana growers lobbying for price supports, as in the case of sugar. The government in Ecuador *would* feel a responsibility to help the growers, but would be unable to seek a government-to-government solution because of the American position on private enterprise.

Advanced industrialized countries too now have occasion to pay more attention to the rationale of the international economic system as interdependence has forced them also to experience the dependency side of international life. The club which finally gained the mule's attention was the profound economic shock caused by skyrocketing crude oil prices in the 1970s. The world monetary system itself was thrown off balance as unprecedented sums shifted to the control of previously relatively passive oil states. All the assumptions on which the international economic system were based were shaken. This threw calculations about many international issues into confusion.

Thus, changes in the system force new attention to be paid to the underlying assumptions of the system itself. For instance, consider the entry of a new kind of player on the scene—multinational corporations. While perhaps not really new, their increasing number and their "global reach," to use the title of Richard Barnet and Ronald Muller's book on the subject, alter the function of the system.[3] They are subject to no uniform set of national laws and regulations, but rather operate at the interface of such laws. Furthermore, they carry their own rationale. In effect, it can be argued that multinational corporations are the cutting edge for a truly international economic system by providing an international means for interconnecting goods and services that would not be possible with national-level enterprises, each seeking their own way in the complex of international economic forces. These corporations think in terms of an international labor force, an international market, international use of resources, even their own monetary systems based on corporation transfers of funds and internationalized accounting systems. It is a system that blurs national economic and even political boundaries. It forces a new pattern of reasoning onto the international economy.

Information control. Still another development that is forcing change in the way everyone will have to think about the international economic system is the fact that world society is becoming increasingly an information society. That is, an increasing portion of economic activity involves the creation, processing and transmission of information. All parts of the international system are increasingly dependent on information flows, from the sharing of technology and fundamental reliance on data banks to the complex communication by which modern enterprises operate.

Control of information and its use gives any country an advantage in the system, and at the present the United States is the largest producer, consumer and exporter of information of all kinds, including entertainment and television programming. The importance of all this to the U.S. is seen in the fact that when the World Administrative Radio Conference—the international body that regulates use of the radio waves spectrum and international communication practices—met in Geneva in 1979, the United States fielded the largest delegation to an international conference in its history. The importance of information technology and its production can hardly be overestimated as a force reshaping the economic order. Hence, part of the demand for a new international economic order includes a call for equity in access to new information technology.

We would hope that all this discussion suggests an urgency in making some progress in the broad application of mindset analysis to international economic processes. For again, in economics as in political and other world affairs, it is not just what the economic facts are, but what people *think* they are and what they mean, that is often the essential consideration. We lag well behind in understanding this facet of international economics.

Coping with the Mindset Dimension

If the direction of inquiry that has been urged in the preceding chapters has the merit that is argued, how, in practical application, do we get on with it?

As international practitioners—which most of us are to a degree—we have a vested interest both personally and collectively in increasing competence in addressing the psycho-cultural factors that are critical for coping in our international interaction. In effect, while we are now managing many aspects of our international operations with great sophistication, we still tend to leave the key psycho-cultural dimension unattended. We operate by hunch and by habit, profiting only inefficiently from cumulative experience because we lack a clear frame of reference for learning from it. In our international activities we need to take some of the mystery out of the contrasts in mindsets that we encounter. We need that sense of security that comes with the ability to anticipate reactions and predict outcomes. To resolve problems we have to decrease the range of factors which seem capricious, intangible, or out of control.

It helps when professionals, in diagnosing cross-national issues, can find a way to stand back objectively from the action and get a detached view of what is going on in the interaction and communication that is an integral part of their programs or projects. But along with a detached perspective, they also need to develop the ability to recognize when contrasting mindsets are at work. This calls for an acuteness in on-the-spot observational skills which allows the practitioner to sift through the raw materials of ordinary experience in a foreign country and put together the elements, like pieces of a puzzle, to capture the underlying beliefs, assumptions, concerns, and values that give logic and coherence to behavior observed and explain problems that arise in trying to bridge perceptions.

This task may sound like it belongs in the preserve of trained social scientists. But at this stage of international practice, one must be one's own practical psychologist and cultural anthropologist, at least to some degree. If what has been said in this book up to this point works in application, then it is not too formidable an undertaking. At the least, anyone seriously engaged in international practice is regularly going to be making psychological and cultural judgments of some kind. What we offer is the prospect of increasing effectiveness, of making one's experience cumulative and, over time, of enabling one to become the person with ten years of experience rather than the person with one year's experience ten times.

Therefore, this chapter, while also serving as something of a summary, proposes eight general considerations for the practitioner's agenda for increasing observational and diagnostic skills when dealing with the mindset factor.

COMMITMENT TO EMPHASIZING MINDSET FACTORS

First is the matter of emphasis. We have to take the probability of mismatched mindsets more seriously in the many phases of our international activities. Probing mindsets has to become standard operating procedure in international decision making, negotiating, project planning, and strategy development. In international operations it is already routine to study laws and regulations, costs and economic projections, political risks, vested interest conflicts, and so forth. Indeed, research departments focused on there areas are often available to support overseas operations. At least as much purposeful effort needs to go into the psycho-cultural dimension.

This is a potentially exciting subject for innovation, but it does mean discarding some old approaches and analytical habits. At the organizational level, it means institutionalizing a new element in the planning and conducting of international business. At the personal level, it means an enhanced competence. Hopefully, it will become "old-fashioned" to venture abroad without it.

MINDSET ANALYSIS AS A CENTRAL FOCUS IN AREA AND COUNTRY STUDIES

Secondly, there are implications for the way we prepare for overseas assignments. The need to understand outlooks and perceptions can serve as a central focus or rationale for area and country studies.

It is accepted as only prudent to "read up" on the place to which one has been assigned. Geography, history, the people and culture, current affairs, and other such subjects are pursued both to provide a background and to enhance one's enjoyment of the venture. Special briefings may be provided along with counsel on the "dos and don'ts" for getting along. If one wants to specialize further, universities provide area and country studies, even advanced degrees. However, at whatever the level of effort, the tendency is simply to accumulate facts and descriptive detail with very little systematic sense of objective or method for organizing the gathered facts into usable patterns.

The thesis here is that an effort to learn how to capture prevailing mindsets could serve as the integrating rationale for pursuing area and country study. One should ask, as one accumulates knowledge about a country, how each piece of information contributes to a way of thinking, how the circumstances of the society and the culture that has evolved molds the personality patterns of the people who have been socialized in its ways. Such could be the central thread to be discovered in the course of one's background study, a thread that could continue to be pursued throughout a stay in the country itself. Such a sense of objective would provide the focus for what otherwise might be a smorgasbord or dilettante mode of learning.

USING LANGUAGE STUDY TO CAPTURE MINDSETS

In line with what was said earlier about language and perception, there is a need to expand the sense of objective in language study to try to bridge mindsets rather than simply match words. It can be argued that too often people learn a foreign language for the wrong reason, or at least for an insufficient reason. The larger purpose is communication, and language, especially when approached as a mechanical tool or worse yet as computer-assisted translation, is only one aspect of this. The reason for learning a foreign language should go beyond the ability to order meals and direct taxis, practically helpful though that might be. Language is an essential part of communication, but it is not communication itself until meaning is assigned to linguistic symbols. What one really wants to do is gain an entré into the thought patterns of the people who speak the language.

So, in the often considerable effort expended in learning a language, the obvious thing is to keep the objective clear. For it is the *subjective* meaning of words and expressions that needs to be captured. Time spent exploring why a given utterance does not translate well may be more productive for the one who is actually trying to communicate than concentration on technical excellence. All this suggests for most students, and often for teachers as well, a more sophisticated sense of objective in language learning. There is much to be gained in the area where linguistic science, anthropology and social psychology meet.

In general, the tendency to emphasize language programs as the single most important factor in achieving mutual understanding needs reconsideration. I recall two separate cases of Americans working in Latin America in which the ability to learn the language was not the basic problem. The problem was that these two people had virtually no ability to empathize with the locals, that is, no basis for *communication*. In one case, a woman with a technical competence in Spanish that was unmatched by anyone in her group became a continuing public relations problem as she managed to irritate everyone with egocentric precision. In the other case, a man in the third year of his assignment was still unable to speak Spanish even in the simplest terms. But because of what he *would* have said had he been able, he gave me almost daily cause to be thankful that he could *not* put his thoughts into Spanish! It might also be noted that in the first situation another woman who was unable to make any progress in Spanish nevertheless became one of the most popular members of the team; the real empathy she wanted to communicate came through despite the lack of words.

In sum, preoccupation with the mechanics of a foreign language should not be allowed to interfere with communication. Primary attention should go to the larger aspects of communication. In fact, much would be gained by preparing special short communication courses for the many people who will *not* be able to dedicate the time necessary for gaining real fluency in the language of their area of assignment. This would be especially germane for the so-called "hard" languages, such as Chinese and Hindi. The course would then become, for instance, "Communicating with the Chinese." It might include some basic language content, but much more emphasis would be placed on total patterns of communication, on the nature of the language as related to culture and thought, and on the way that people who speak it relate to each other. It could cover a range from the meaning of courtesies—the cultural rationale behind exchanging calling cards in China, for example—to elements of social structure, values, and implicit philosophy. At the very least, such a course would leave the student much better prepared to use interpreters and to judge intended meaning when counterparts speak the visitor's language as a second language.

SHARPENING CULTURE-LEARNING SKILLS

When in a foreign environment, one needs to sharpen one's observational skills, for after all, contrasting mindsets are all around. The skill involved is not only observing *what* is going on, but exploring the *why* behind the behavior. If what one observes is routinely repeated, it is almost certainly a cultural pattern. The values of a culture can be detected by observing such things as who are considered heroes and who villains, how people deal with each other in various relationships, who is praised or condemned in the newspapers and why, what themes come up in local songs, literature, myths, and children's stories and textbooks. Values are reflected in idioms, maxims and proverbs, in taboos and laws and in the behavior that evokes emotional responses. The problem is to put them together in patterns.

Part of the culture-learning task is a matter of finding reliable interpreters of the local culture. One's compatriot, "the old hand," might or might *not* be useful or reliable in this role. On the other hand, one's local friends might not be able to offer the explanations needed either, for what the outsider needs to understand is simply common sense to them—they are likely to have little practice in articulating or explaining it. In some cases reliable literature is available or competent cross-cultural specialists are able to offer valuable insights. But even the best of insights may need adaptation to changing conditions or to specific culture groups.

Happily, this culture-learning skill, once acquired, is transferrable as one goes from one country to another. But it has to be a conscious, intellectual approach in which *you* are in charge. This is a different order of adaptation to a foreign environment than simply gathering information and advice from someone else. One has to build up one's own understanding of why behavior is what it is and how it fits into the larger cultural system.

DETERMINING THE STRESS POINTS IN DEALING WITH CONTRASTING MINDSETS

Perhaps the most challenging objective, and one that pays the highest dividends in making sense of intercultural communication problems, is to determine which aspects of deep culture tend to be the most difficult to bridge. In effect, as one thinks of constructing a communication bridge with counterparts of another culture, one must, as an architect, determine the *stress points* which demand the most support if the bridge is to withstand its load. Similarly, in cross-cultural contexts, it is useful to focus on those critical mismatches in mindsets which typically affect communication for a given cross-cultural relationship. This is especially important when the subject matter is abstract, as project plans, government policies, laws or institutionalized activities usually are.

For example, differing conceptions of time might constitute a stress point, depending on the importance of time to the issue or interaction of the moment. In getting equipment repaired on a construction project, time might be crucial; in other contexts it might not actually be a stress point. When Americans work overseas in technical assistance programs, the contrast between the fatalistic orientation often encountered in the local peasantry and the activism and optimism of the American technicians would be a probable cross-cultural stress point. Or, in U.S.-Japanese management relations, a stress point might emerge when differing views of the role individuals play in organizations result in communication or other kinds of breakdowns. In some situations, contrasting values relative to youth and age might affect attitudes toward leadership and decision making—age, for instance, is imbued with more authority and respect in the Orient than in the West.

Although it may seem difficult to grasp this level of culture and relate it to the way real people behave, it is the essence of the mindset inquiry and cannot be avoided. In actual situations we make some kind of judgments regarding deep culture all the time, even when we unconsciously project the assumption that our own way of thinking is universal—or should be. The problem is to increase the cross-cultural accuracy of our judgments. One of the keys in advancing one's interpretive skills in this regard is to maintain awareness of the implicit assumptions and philosophical orientations of one's own culture. That will usually address half of the problem.

CONTRASTS IN THE INFORMATION BASE

Looking for contrasts in the information bases that contribute to your and your counterpart's mindsets should be routine. This is one of the easier things to do. One takes the content of the local press and media seriously and analyzes it carefully (and does the same with one's own press and media). It is almost always useful to become better acquainted with the local educational system, both for what is taught and how it is interpreted. The local society itself can be viewed as an information flow system as one tries to understand whose opinions count, who the opinion leaders and persuaders are, or whose judgment is deferred to. The objective is to be able to diagnose mindsets in terms of the information bases that help explain them.

THE BICULTURAL PERSONALITY

There is good reason to be more analytically respectful of people with bicultural personalities. In many situations, international work will not involve coping with foreign mindsets directly, but interacting through interpreters, through host nationals whose mission it is to deal with outsiders, or through members of one's own organization with extended experience in the country in question. It is important to understand how such people, from a psycho-cultural perspective, go back and forth from one pattern of thinking to another and from one identity to another.

These are people who have had substantial experience in more than one culture; they speak second and third languages or more, and in their normal routines have occasion to interact with other people in varying cultural frames of reference. Many people start out with bicultural personalities to some degree if they have come from homes which retain distinct ethnic identities or have worked or lived abroad. In effect, such people are operating with more than one computer in their heads, and it is not easy, especially if the cultures they have experienced are ones with great fundamental differences in underlying deep cultural attributes.

Not only do such people serve as buffers between conflicting mindsets, they can provide insight into ongoing communication problems. A sensitive observer can learn much by simply watching them switch approaches as they move from one cultural context to another. They can also be good advisors and teachers if they are at ease with their bicultural (or multicultural) selves and are able to articulate the logic of their bi- or multiculturalism.

Sometimes, in dealing with these cultural brokers, one needs to judge the degree to which they are actually competent in bridging cultures within their own cognitive systems. For example, might your Russian counterpart be speaking English but thinking Russian? (Or, for that matter, might the American, despite long residence abroad, be speaking the local language but still be thinking American?) If bicultural people are not able to maintain a stable and satisfying balance in their identities, as, for example, in Third World cases in which a "native" image is repressed in an attempt to take on the greater prestige of a more modern or Western self-image, the cross-cultural bridging function they might provide can go askew. As more and more international business is conducted through a rapidly developing overlay of international culture, with which people unsatisfied with their own cultural circumstances sometimes avidly identify, this problem is likely to arise more frequently.

The point here is that if one is to cope with contrasting mindsets, more thoughtful attention needs to be directed toward the bicultural phenomenon. In simpler and more provincial times, when people traveled infrequently and dealt with people of other cultures only as immiscible aliens, there was little occasion to consider the dynamics of dealing with bicultural personalities.

Now, most people with any cosmopolitan pretensions find themselves socialized to some extent in more than one culture; they expand the complications of their thought patterns accordingly.

While all this poses many strains in personality integration that remain largely unstudied, the existence of multicultural personalities is ultimately an extremely important international asset. International problem solving depends on a multiplication of just such people—the true internationalists. And while most people will want to retain their own basic cultural identity, absorbing other cultures to the degree that one remains an integrated personality is a valid objective for anyone who wants to work effectively and happily abroad.

The task is to stay in charge of what is happening as one inevitably absorbs bits of a foreign culture. For if culture is learned and socially-shared thinking and behavior, it can be taken up by newcomers simply in day-to-day experience. The difficulty lies in identifying and learning the design and logic that goes with the second culture rather than simply bumbling along with an undigested collection of disparate new habits to which one has become enured. When one learns a culture as a child, the "common sense" of a culture is absorbed and remains largely out of awareness. When people enter a new culture later in life, their original common sense remains imprinted indelibly in their psyches to block the new, so they have to apply greater intellectual effort to capture the web and logic of the second culture.

To the extent that one can succeed in this effort, the sense of personal security in living abroad goes up as does one's effectiveness. The so-called culture shock that affects people trying to adapt to a new cultural environment is in large part a matter of being cut off from all the familiar cues and sense of design inherent in the web of one's own culture and suddenly finding oneself unable to predict or make sense of what is going on. This deprivation is wearing and leaves one disoriented—hence, the shock. The cure is to be able to absorb the new sense of cultural logic so that behavior no longer seems capricious and unpredictable. Even if one still does not like the new ways, they will generate less anxiety and coping will be facilitated. At this point, one is becoming a bicultural personality.

RESEARCH AND DEVELOPMENT

Finally, the agenda for coping with the mindset dimension calls for the kind of research and development already applied in other aspects of international affairs. As international practitioners gain more experience in pursuing psychological and cross-cultural considerations, they should be able to articulate priorities for applied social science research aimed at a deeper and more reliable understanding of psycho-cultural factors in international practice. In pursuit of this objective, our collective competence rides on the ability of anthropologists, sociologists, social psychologists and linguistic and communication scientists, among others, to engage in multidisciplinary applied projects.

What has been done so far is modest but important. There are precedents in approaches taken in technical assistance programs and to some extent in international management. A start has been made in the international relations field in studying psycho-cultural aspects of political and social change, although the field of international economics has been slower in taking into account work done on psychological and cultural variables in economic processes. There has been considerable activity in training for international work. However, much of the training effort has concentrated more on techniques than on applying basic theory and concepts.

Such countries as are able to channel research and development energies in this direction can be expected to enjoy a substantial advantage as a larger portion of any nation's problems becomes international in scope. While a greater comprehension of the role the mindset factor plays will not be a panacea for resolving all conflict, it will help decrease the damage caused by misperception and misattribution of motives which, left running amok, compounds the difficulty in all international problem solving and conflict resolution.

References

CHAPTER ONE

1. A point stressed in Kenneth Boulding's classic study, *The Image: Knowledge in Life and Society,*, University of Michigan Press, 1956. A later pioneer was Joseph H. de Rivera, *The Psychological Dimension of Foreign Policy,* Merrill, 1968.

2. For the decision making process in operation at this time, see Barry Rubin, *Secrets of State: The State Department and the Struggle Over U.S. Foreign Policy,* Oxford Press, 1985.

3. Elaborated in more detail in Glen Fisher, *Public Diplomacy and the Behavioral Sciences,* Indiana University Press, 1972.

4. A consideration emphasized for the academic community in Graham T. Allison, *Essence of Decision,* Little, Brown and Co., 1971.

5. Transaction Books, 1980.

6. See discussion by Stephen F. Cohen, *Rethinking the Soviet Experience: Politics and History Since 1917,* Oxford University Press, 1985.

7. Holt, Rinehart and Winston, 1965. See also the summary collection that did much to define the field of Political Psychology: Jeanne N. Knutson (ed.), *Handbook of Political Psychology,* Jossey-Bass, 1973.

8. For one summary, see Stephen G. Walker and Timothy G. Murphy, "The Utility of the Operational Code in Political Forecasting," *Political Psychology,* 1982, Vol. 3, No. 1 & 2, pp. 24-60.

9. Westover Press, 1980.

10. Random House, 1971. (Fourth Edition, 1986)

11. Houghton Mifflin, 1972,

12. Princeton University Press, 1976.

CHAPTER TWO

1. For one introductory summary of concepts in social psychology, see Daryl J. Bem, *Beliefs, Attitudes, and Human Affairs*, Wadsworth Publishing Co. (Brooks/Cole), 1970. Or see the summary of basics in Joseph H. de Rivera, *The Psychological Dimension of Foreign Policy*, Merrill, 1968, Ch. 2. For perception and the way it is related to culture, see first three chapters of Marshall R. Singer, *Intercultural Communication: A Perceptual Approach.* Prentice-Hall, 1986.

2. For a condensed summary of this idea applied to foreign affairs analysis, see Martha L. Cottam, "The Impact of Psychological Images on International Bargaining: The Case of Mexican Natural Gas," *Political Psychology*, 1985, Vol. 6, No. 3, pp. 413-440. For a more complete study, see the same author's *Foreign Policy Decision Making: The Influence of Cognition*, Westview Press, 1986.

3. The Exploratorium science museum in San Francisco contains a version of the Cantril room.

4. A classic study that explored such facets of Japanese personality was Ruth Benedict's *The Chrysanthemum and the Sword*, Houghton Mifflin, 1946, which is still read with interest by both Americans and Japanese despite the dated picture it presents and the fact that the entire study was done from the distant vantage point of the United States during wartime. For a more recent source, see Takie Sugiyama Lebra, *Japanese Patterns of Behavior*, University of Hawaii Press, 1976.

5. Anthony Marc Lewis, "The Blind Spot of U.S. Foreign Intelligence," *Journal of Communication*, Winter, 1976, Vol. 26, No. 1, pp. 44-54.

6. Les Aspin, "Misreading Intelligence," *Foreign Policy*, Summer, 1981, Vol. 43, pp. 166-172.

7. Oxford University Press, 1985.

8. The Free Press, 1984.

9. For a review of this problem and current theory as related to decision making, see Alexander George, *Presidential Decision-making in Foreign Policy: The Effective Use of Information and Advice*, Westview Press, 1980.

10. Houghton Mifflin, 1972.

11. Again, see Alexander George, *op. cit.* This is the main thrust of his study of presidential decision making.

12. For my own longer review of the relationship between language and perception, see Glen H. Fisher, *Public Diplomacy and the Behavioral Sciences,*, Indiana University Press, 1972, Ch. 5. The references to Whorf come from Benjamin Lee Whorf, *Language, Thought and Reality*, M.I.T. Press, 1964.

CHAPTER THREE

1. See Stanley Hoffman, "Perception, Reality and the Franco-American Conflict," *Journal of International Affairs*, 1967, Vol. XXI, No. 1. For another look at European national characteristics as related to international cooperation, see Luigi Barzini, *The Europeans*, Simon and Schuster, 1983.

2. As reported in interviews conducted for the study: Glen Fisher, *International Negotiation: A Cross-Cultural Perspective*, Intercultural Press, 1982.

3. Princeton University Press, 1976.

4. Princeton University Press, 1976.

5. This would be borne out, for example, in the collection of articles in Lawrence S. Falkowski, *Psychological Models in World Politics*, Westview Press, 1979.

6. Much of this as presented was adapted from my earlier *Public Diplomacy and the Behavioral Sciences*, Indiana University Press, 1972. For a more penetrating analysis of American value orientations see Edward C.

Stewart and Milton Bennett, *American Cultural Patterns: A Cross-Cultural Perspective*, Revised edition, Intercultural Press, 1987.

7. Considered a classic for early attention to aspects of cross-cultural communication: Edward T. Hall, *The Silent Language*, Doubleday, 1959.

8. An innovative authority on patterns of reasoning, especially as it applies to international affairs, is Edmund S. Glenn. See especially his summary work *Man and Mankind: Conflict and Communication Between Cultures*, Ablex, 1981.

9. The basic source is David D. McClelland, *The Achieving Society*, Princeton University Press, 1961. See also McClelland and David C. Winter, *Motivating Economic Achievement*, Free Press, 1969.

10. Glen Caudill Dealy, *The Public Man—An Interpretation of Latin American and Other Catholic Countries*, University of Massachusetts Press, 1977.

CHAPTER FOUR

1. Leon Wolff, *Little Brown Brothers*, Doubleday, 1960.

2. See the Asia Society's summary, *Asia in American Textbooks*, New York, 1976.

3. As in the last chapter, an important reference is Edmund Glenn, *Man and Mankind: Conflict and Communication Between Cultures*, Ablex, 1981. In relation to negotiation, the problem is summarized in Glen Fisher, *International Negotiation: A Cross-Cultural Perspective*, Intercultural Press, 1982. pp. 49-52.

CHAPTER FIVE

1. Rusk as reported by *The Washington Post*, July 3, 1971.

2. See *New York Times*, January 13, 1982, p. 5.

3. This perspective is summarized by Alex Inkeles, Eugenia Hanfmann and Helen Beir in "Model Personality and Adjustment to the Soviet Socio-Political System," in Bert Kaplan (ed.) *Studying Personality Cross-Culturally*, Harper & Row, 1961.

4. See *The Washington Post*, for example, December 9, 1981, p. A11.

5. This idea was developed in various of Weber's works and enlarged upon by followers. For a basic statement, see Max Weber, "The Three Types of Legitimate Rule," in the reader edited by Marcello Truzzi, *Sociology: The Classic Statements*, Random House, 1971.

6. A particularly penetrating study of the persistence of thought patterns regarding government function, power and privilege is provided in Jeffrey W. Barrett, *The Impulse to Revolution in Latin America*, Praeger, 1985.

7. From James A. Michener's account in *Iberia: Spanish Travels and Reflections*, Random House, 1968, p. 56.

8. Credit for the start of an extended literature on images and perception is usually given to Walter Lippmann, whose book *Public Opinion*, published in 1922, talked about "pictures in our heads." Harcourt Brace.

9. New York University Press, 1986. See also the critical article with extended bibliography: James G. Blight, "How Might Psychology Contribute to Reducing the Risk of Nuclear War?" *Political Psychology*, Vol. 7, No. 4, 1986.

10. There is a growing literature on international news flow. My own contribution is contained in Glen Fisher, *American Communication in a Global Society*, Revised edition, Ablex, 1987,

CHAPTER SIX

1. Everett G. Martin, "What Does a Nation Do If It's Out to Win a Nobel Prize or Two?" as headlined in the *Wall Street Journal*, Feb. 10, 1981.

2. Lawrence E. Harrison, *Underdevelopment is a State of Mind: The Latin American Case*, The Center for International Affairs, Harvard University, and University Press of America, 1985. Also, for a more detailed case regarding cultural factors in the modernization process, see Jeffrey W. Barrett, *The Impulse to Revolution in Latin America*, Praeger, 1985.

3. Much of the work done on American values is summarized in Edward C. Stewart and Milton Bennett, *American Cultural Patterns: A Cross-Cultural Perspective*, Revised edition, Intercultural Press, 1987.

4. See David D. McClelland, *The Achieving Society,* Van Nostrand, 1961, and McClelland and David G. Winter, *Motivating Economic Achievement,* The Free Press, 1969.

5. Tomas Roberto Fillol, *Social Factors in Economic Development: The Argentine Case,* MIT Press, 1961.

6. *Ibid.*

7. Harper and Row, 1962.

CHAPTER SEVEN

1. Robert B. Reich's book *The Next American Frontier,* Times Books, 1983, prompted considerable discussion at the higher levels of politics and business as he stressed that "paper entrepreneuralism" was a counterproductive trend in the U.S. economy's attempt to compete in the world economic system.

2. Gene Gregory, *The Logic of Japanese Enterprise,* Business Series No. 92, Sophia University Institute of Comparative Culture (Tokyo), 1982. This is the theme much more specifically elaborated in David Halberstam's *The Reckoning,* William Morrow and Co., 1986, and in Akio Morita's *Made in Japan,* E.P. Dutton, 1986.

3. Richard J. Barnet and Ronald E. Muller, *Global Reach: The Power of the Multinational Corporation,* Simon and Schuster, 1974.

Index